# PUZZLELOPEDIA

# PUZZLE

Mind-Bending,
Brain-Teasing
Word Games,
Picture Puzzles,
Mazes, and More!

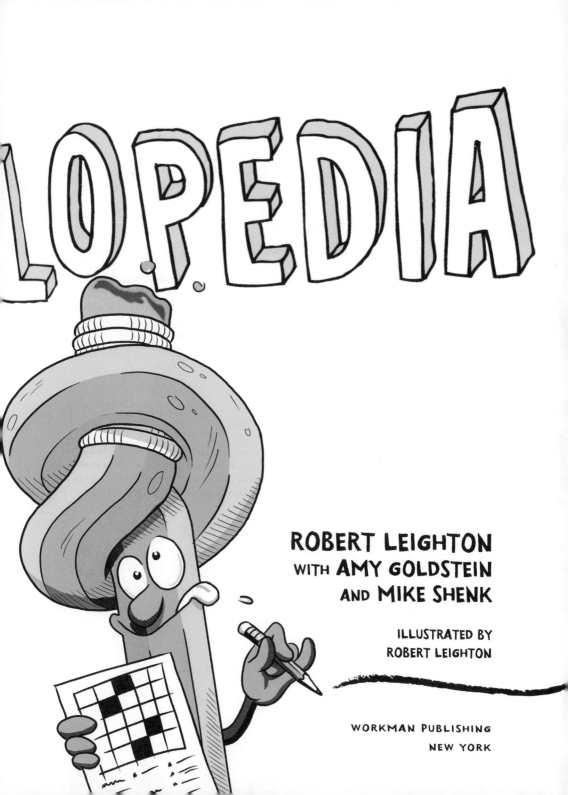

# LOPEDIA

**ROBERT LEIGHTON**
WITH **AMY GOLDSTEIN**
AND **MIKE SHENK**

ILLUSTRATED BY
ROBERT LEIGHTON

WORKMAN PUBLISHING
NEW YORK

Library of Congress Cataloging-in-Publication Data is available.

ISBN 978-0-7611-7220-8

Design by Maria Elias

Workman books are available at special discounts when purchased in bulk for premiums and sales promotions as well as for fund-raising or educational use. Special editions or book excerpts can also be created to specification. For details, contact the Special Sales Director at the address below, or send an email to specialmarkets@workman.com.

Workman Publishing Co., Inc.
225 Varick Street
New York, NY 10014-4381
workman.com

Printed in China

First printing July 2019

10  9  8  7  6  5  4  3  2  1

# PUZZLELOPEDIA

# WHAT YOU NEED TO KNOW ABOUT THIS PUZZLE BOOK

# INTRODUCTION

**WELCOME TO** PUZZLELOPEDIA, **YOUR A-TO-Z PUZZLE COLLECTION.** Puzzles are meant to be solved, so switch on your solving brain and dive right in. Within these pages are a few puzzle types you might have seen before (crosswords, mazes, sudoku) and many that you haven't (Frankenwords, Pinwheel, Zigs and Zags).

You'll also find special "Puzzle Breakers" highlighting some of the entertaining, curious, or surprising ways people play with words, pictures, and cornfields. (Cornfields? See page 108.) Along the way, you'll have your brain teased, tickled, and irreversibly stretched. Maybe you'll be the first kid on your block to write a pangram. (A pangram? See page 134.)

**Before you get started, here are a few words of advice:**

**1** **JUST AS YOU WOULDN'T READ AN ENCYCLOPEDIA FROM A TO Z,** you don't have to solve *Puzzlelopedia* from front to back. The puzzles are organized in alphabetical order, but that doesn't mean you have to start with A. Flip through, find a puzzle that looks fun, and start there. It's your book—solve it in any order you like.

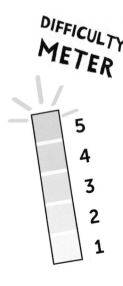

DIFFICULTY METER

5
4
3
2
1

**2** NEXT TO EVERY PUZZLE, THERE'S A DIFFICULTY METER TO GIVE YOU SOME IDEA OF WHAT TO EXPECT. You'll find that some puzzles start out seeming difficult but are actually pretty easy once you get the hang of solving them. Others have lots of parts and though some parts are easy, some are not. One thing is for certain: The more puzzles you solve, the better you'll get.

**3** READ THE INSTRUCTIONS CAREFULLY BEFORE YOU GET STARTED. Will all the answers start with a particular letter? What is the purpose of the shaded boxes? How can this be a maze when it doesn't even have paths? Every puzzle has rules, and reading the instructions (as well as checking them again while you're solving) will make things go more smoothly. If something doesn't seem to make sense, reread the instructions. They may even include a freebie answer you can use as an example.

### 4 IF YOU GET STUCK ON A PUZZLE, SET IT ASIDE.

There are more than 200 puzzles in *Puzzlelopedia*, and they're all waiting to be solved. If you can't finish the one you're working on, leave it and come back to it later. Your next move may suddenly seem obvious. In the meantime, you might want to use a pencil with an eraser!

Now that you have everything you need to get started, are you ready to dive in? Grab that pencil, choose your letter, and start solving!

### OH WAIT—THE ANSWERS!

They're all in the back, in alphabetical order—just like the puzzles.

# THE PUZZLES

 # THE PUZZLE.

This a-shaped grid has entries reading left, right, up, down, and diagonally. The letter A is the only vowel in each word. To earn an A, find all the words, ignoring spaces between words. Then read the leftover letters from left to right, starting with the top row, to discover a Bonus Message about a place with even *more* A words.

| | |
|---|---|
| AARDVARK | LLAMA |
| ABRACADABRA | MA'AM |
| ALARM | MADAGASCAR |
| ALAS | MAGMA |
| ALMANAC | MAMA |
| ARTS AND CRAFTS | MANGA |
| AVATAR | NASA |
| AWARD | PANAMA CANAL |
| BABAR | PANDA |
| BACKPACK | PAPA |
| BANANAGRAMS | PARKA |
| BATMAN | PASTA |
| CARAVAN | RADAR |
| CAR WASH | RAP STAR |
| DRAMA | RAZZMATAZZ |
| FLASH CARDS | SALSA |
| HANGMAN | SANTA |
| HASHTAG | SNACK BAR |
| KWANZAA | STAR WARS |
| LASAGNA | TARZAN |
| LAVA | WALMART |

```
          K C A P K C A B
      A M W A M R A D A R N A
    S L H A N G M A N A R A R T
    A A L N A A A N S A H W B A
  S N R A Z Z M A T A Z Z A A A J
  A T M P A A         V N R D S B
  P A S T A           A D A C H
                      R R C T A
        N A A W A L M A R T
      A A D V A S M A A L R C F
    K A S M A R G A N A N A B A L
  S R L T T K A A N R A A K A N A
  L A S A G N A A       C A L A S
  S V R R N             A K S M H
  A D H W L             M S B L C
  B R M A A       L L A M A A A
  N A V R S T F A R C D N A S T R A
    A T S H H A K T T A A N G A D P
    M A M A N T R A T S P A R N S A
      D R A C S A G A D A M A A A P
        T N L P G     A P N T A M
```

3

## BONUS MESSAGE:

__ _____ ___ _____,
_____, _____, _____,
_____, ___ _____.

# ADDITION EDITION

Describe each of these scenes with two words. The second word is the same as the first word *plus* one additional letter. For example, a drawing of a calendar page with a butterfly-like insect would be a MOTH MONTH. Can you figure out the names of all the pictures?

1

2    _ _ _ _ _<br>    _ _ _ _ _

1    _ _ _<br>   _ _ _ _

3    _ _ _ _ _<br>   _ _ _ _ _ _

4    _ _ _ _<br>   _ _ _ _ _

5    _ _ _ _<br>   _ _ _ _ _

6    _ _ _ _ _<br>   _ _ _ _ _ _

# AHA!

To find the answer to the riddle, first use the clues to fill in the grids. The answers are the same both across and down, so enter each word in both directions. When you've filled in all the words, use the symbols to transfer those letters to the boxes below to spell the riddle's answer.

**Q:** Where did Sir Isaac Newton get his best ideas?

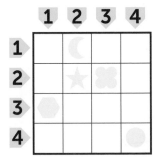

1 Female spouse

2 It's symbolized by a light bulb over the head

3 Touched with the fingertips

4 Has a meal

---

1 Pleasant conversation

2 Wish for

3 Gorillas and orangutans

4 Exam at the end of a unit

# ALL THOSE OPPOSED

First, write the opposite of each word on the blanks beside it. All the opposites in each group have something in common with each other—except for one, which doesn't belong with the others in the group. When you have finished all three groups, follow the instructions at the bottom of the page to get the final answer.

## GROUP 1

Wet / _ _ _ _

In / _ _ _ _

Difficult / _ _ _ _ _

Beautiful / _ _ _ _ _

Night / _ _ _ _

Innocent / _ _ _ _ _ _ _

Full / _ _ _ _ _ _

## GROUP 2

Rich / _ _ _ _ _

My / _ _ _ _ _

Ceiling / _ _ _ _ _ _

Against / _ _ _ _ _

Peace / _ _ _ _

Even / _ _ _ _

Less / _ _ _ _ _

## GROUP 3

Always / _ _ _ _ _ _ _

Shallow / _ _ _ _ _

Absent / _ _ _ _ _ _ _ _

Woman / _ _ _ _

Sour / _ _ _ _ _ _

Worse / _ _ _ _ _ _ _

Forget / _ _ _ _ _ _ _ _

**Now rearrange the three misfit words to get an appropriate final phrase:**

A: _____  _____  _____

6

# ALPHA-CROSS

Use each letter of the alphabet just once to complete the grid. Although some spaces could contain different letters, there is only one way to complete the entire grid.

A B C D E F G H I J K L M N O P Q R S T U V W X Y Z

# AMPERSANDWICHES

Each string of letters contains two words often joined by an &, like BOW & ARROW. In each string, the letters of each word are in order, but intermingled with the letters of the other. For example, SFAQUIARRE would lead to the answer FAIR & SQUARE. Can you unscramble the pairs below?

| 1 | SHIEEDKE | _____ & _____ |
| 2 | NEPEIDLNESS | _____ & _____ |
| 3 | STHOELWL | _____ & _____ |
| 4 | SSUPIGACRE | _____ & _____ |
| 5 | LCOLEAURD | _____ & _____ |
| 6 | TLHIUGNHTDNIENGR | _____ & _____ |
| 7 | CMAHECEARSOENI | _____ & _____ |

# ANAGRAMS

## WHY A DORMITORY IS A DIRTY ROOM

### The eyes—they see.

**T**hat's true, of course, but look again. THE EYES contains *exactly* the same letters as THEY SEE. That's an *anagram*: a rearrangement of all the letters in one word or phrase to spell another word or phrase.

The best anagrams say something about the original concept instead of just scrambling the letters to spell something random. The letters in DORMITORY can be rearranged to spell lots of different phrases: I DRY MOTOR, RID MY ROOT, I'D TRY MOOR. But by far the best is DIRTY ROOM, which is a pretty good description of a dormitory.

Of all forms of wordplay, anagrams may be the most delightful. It can be amazing to discover that ANGERED becomes ENRAGED. ASTRONOMER becomes MOON STARER. STATUE OF LIBERTY? BUILT TO STAY FREE!

Some anagrams, called *antigrams*, are opposites of each other. Two examples are UNTIED and UNITED, and WITHIN EARSHOT and I WON'T HEAR THIS.

Anagrams show up in places you might not expect—or even notice. Japan's old capital city, KYOTO, and its current capital city, TOKYO, are anagrams of each other. Matt Groening, who created the TV show *The Simpsons*, says that he named the boy BART because it was an anagram of BRAT. In 1998, a former NASA aerospace engineer named

Homer Hickam published a book called *Rocket Boys* about how he and his childhood friends took up rocketry after seeing a satellite one October night. The following year the book was made into a film, *October Sky*. Both are very good titles for this story. But even better? They're anagrams!

One of the most impressive anagrams ever discovered is this sentence about a salesman who lowers prices: DISCOUNTER INTRODUCES REDUCTIONS. Amazingly, all three words have the same letters.

Try making your own anagrams with a set of Scrabble or Bananagrams tiles (so that's where the name came from!). Anagram your name, or try a favorite title. Here's one to get you started: *PUZZLELOPEDIA* anagrams to PEEL LOUD PIZZA.

The expression TWELVE + ONE can be rearranged to spell another pair of numbers that also add up to 13. Can you find the anagram?

For some puzzles based on anagrams, see Having It Both Ways, Holed-Up Note, Mixed Messages, and Y: The Puzzle.

# ANIMAZING

See if you can find your way through this wild maze. Move left, right, up, or down (but not diagonally) to the next animal only if it is either the same color (black, gray, or yellow) or the same type of animal as the one you're on. Start on the yellow lion in the upper left corner. From there, you may move either to the black lion next to it or to the yellow monkey below it. Keep moving until you reach the black monkey in the bottom right corner.

**START**

**FINISH**

# ART BROKEN

Although these two pictures may seem identical, they're different from each other in nine ways. When you find a difference, draw a straight line connecting the item in the top picture to its changed counterpart in the bottom picture. (You may want to use a ruler.) Each line you draw will cross out two letters. When you're done, the left-over letters (reading left to right, top to bottom) will spell the answer to the riddle.

**Q:** Why should an artist never try to draw with a worn-down pencil?

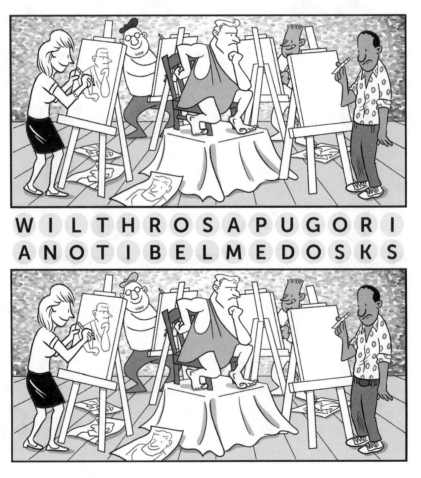

W I L T H R O S A P U G O R I
A N O T I B E L M E D O S K S

**A:** __ __ ' __    __ __ __ __ __ __ __ __ .

# ASTRO-LOGICAL

Chart the skies by mapping out the hidden planets. The total number of planets in each grid is shown below the grid. The numbers along the top and side of each grid tell you how many planets are in that row or column. In addition, each rocket's nose points directly toward a planet. But the planet could be right next to the rocket—or far away! And not every planet will have a rocket pointing to it. You'll find it very useful to know where a planet *can't* go, so when you know a space must be empty, mark it with an X.

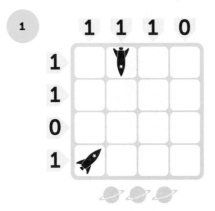

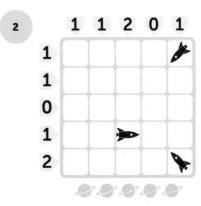

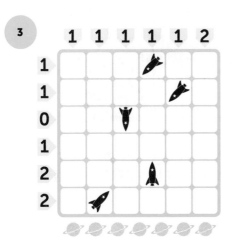

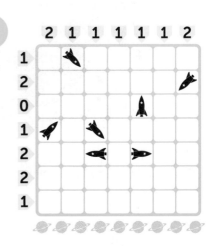

# AUTO MOTIVE

To answer the riddle, look at the ten pieces at the bottom and find them in the large picture. When you find a piece, write the letters showing where it came from—the row first (yellow shield) and the column second (gray shield). When you've found them all, those letters will spell out, in order, the answer to the riddle. The location of the first piece has been filled in for you.

**Q** **Why didn't the police catch whoever stole the tires off their cars?**

**A**: _____

 **THE PUZZLE**

First write the name of each picture. Then cross out the names that can become new words when the letters B-E are added to their beginnings. (For example, you'd cross out TWEEN because it becomes the word BETWEEN.) Three words will be left over. The first and last letters of those words, in the order they appear on the page, will give you the answer to this riddle:

**Q⋮ Why can't an inchworm hang out with snakes?**

**A⋮ Because it will never __ __ __ __ __ __ .**

# BAKER'S DOESN'T

This one should be a piece of cake. Can you find the 27 things that are wrong with this bakery scene?

# BATTER UP!

Write the answer to each clue in the accompanying set of blanks. Each answer will contain BAT or BALL. The yellow B in each answer shows where BAT or BALL begins, but you'll have to figure out which one it is. When you've filled in all the answers, read down one of the columns to find the answer to this riddle:

**Q:** You're locked in a car with nothing but a bat and a ball. How do you get out?

| Clue | Answer |
|---|---|
| Warmed box for chicks to hatch in | |
| Splash-making swimming-pool jump | |
| Very large type of Navy vessel | |
| Common kind of pen | |
| People who do flips, tumbles, and so on | |
| Sport sometimes called "hoops" | |
| What a voter fills out on voting day | |
| Garment you might wear after a shower | |
| Formal argument between "pro" and "con" | |
| Warfare | |
| Spaghetti and _____ | |
| Power source for a toy | |
| Weirdo | |
| Item twirled by someone at the front of the parade | |
| Inflatable items for parties | |
| Woman who might dance in *The Nutcracker* | |

**A:** _ _ _ _ _ _  _ _ _  _ _ _  _ _ _ _.

# BIG DRIPPER

Only two of these gooey ice-cream sundaes are exactly alike. Can you tell which two, and spot the differences among the others?

# BODY BUILDING

You'll have to go out on a limb for this one. Wherever the letters A-R-M or L-E-G appear in the words below, they've been replaced with a picture of an arm or a leg. For example, the word ALLEGIANCE can be found in the grid as AL[leg]IANCE. The words may appear up, down, left, right, or diagonally. (Ignore spaces between words.) When you've circled them all, read the leftover letters (and body parts) from left to right, top to bottom, to get a Bonus Message.

```
Y  M  U  [leg] B  B  U  B  O  W  U  R  V
[arm] Y  O  R  R  S  W  [arm] [leg] M  [arm] [arm] A
Y  [leg] F  M  O  A  C  L  D  L  I  U  S
A  G  N  I  [arm] H  C  E  C  N  I  R  P
S  N  L  E  A  A  E  C  T  L  E  P  E
A  U  A  I  H  E  L  N  [leg] T  S  [leg] [arm]
L  J  R  C  [arm] H  M  A  R  [leg] E  T  I
[arm] O  O  U  O  L  L  I  D  A  [arm] O  N
L  F  F  B  N  U  T  [leg] Y  E  O  O  T
U  F  T  M  I  C  O  L  [leg] E  S  B  A
S  Y  N  N  C  E  T  A  [leg] E  D  O  T
E  R  U  T  A  L  S  I  [leg] R  O  O  M
```

| | | | |
|---|---|---|---|
| ALARM | BOOTLEG | ILLEGAL | PRINCE CHARMING |
| ALLEGIANCE | BUBBLE GUM | JUNGLE GYM | SPEARMINT |
| ANT FARM | COLLEGES | LEGEND | SWARM |
| ARMADILLO | DELEGATE | LEGISLATURE | TELEGRAM |
| ARMCHAIR | EARMUFFS | LEGROOM | VARMINT |
| ARMOR | HARMONICA | MARMALADE | WARM-UP |

## BONUS MESSAGE:

\_\_\_\_  \_\_\_  \_\_  \_\_\_  \_\_\_

\_\_\_  \_\_\_\_\_  \_\_  _____,

\_\_\_  \_\_\_  \_\_\_  \_\_\_.

# BOOK-TAC-TOE

These books form a kind of tic-tac-toe grid. Across each row, down each column, and along both long diagonals, all three books have something in common. It might be something in the titles or in the pictures. Can you figure out all eight?

**ROWS**

**COLUMNS**

**DIAGONALS**

_____     _____     _____

_____     _____     _____

_____     _____     _____

# BRUNCH IS SERVED

## PORTMANTEAU WORDS

The city of London has a reputation for being very foggy. But the city doesn't really experience much fog. The fog that London became known for was actually caused by thick, dirty smoke from coal burned in its factories. It was called *fog* because at the time, there wasn't a word for polluted air. Today, we call it *smog*.

*Smog* was formed by combining the words *smoke* and *fog*. A word made by combining two other words is called a *portmanteau* (port-MAN-toe) word.

There are plenty of words in the English language that were made this way. Some are obvious: *Guesstimate*, for example, is *guess + estimate*; *brunch* = *breakfast* + *lunch*.

But other portmanteau words may surprise you, since they were made by mixing or changing the two combined words. The word *pixel* is a portmanteau of *pix* (short for *pictures*) and *element*. A computer *bit* (a single digit of information) got its name by combining the words *binary digit*. (With only three letters, this may be the shortest portmanteau word ever!)

The original definition of a portmanteau is an old kind of trunk or suitcase that opens into two halves. Lewis Carroll created the newer definition of portmanteau in his book *Through the Looking-Glass*. When the character Alice asks Humpty Dumpty to explain one of the many nonsense words in the poem "Jabberwocky," he tells her, "It's like a portmanteau—there are two meanings packed up into one word."

Carroll was not shy about inventing words when he couldn't find the ones he needed. He introduced the word *chortle* to our language in "Jabberwocky," probably by combining *chuckle* and *snort*. This kind of portmanteau can't be broken into halves; it's more of a meld between two complete words.

And by the way, *meld* is a portmanteau too! It was coined around 1936 by combining the words *melt* and *weld*.

Each of the following pairs of words can be combined in some way to form a familiar portmanteau word. Can you figure out each?

a. Labrador and poodle
b. motor and pedal
c. information and commercial
d. lollipop and icicle
e. internal and communication

# BUG OUT

This puzzle is crawling with bugs. To find them, answer each clue by filling in the squares in each row with the name of an insect.

**1** What you put on a wall using a roller or brush:

P ☐ I ☐ ☐

**2** Hugely successful film:

B ☐ ☐ ☐ K B ☐ ☐ ☐ E R

**3** Contest where competitors try to capture each other's kings:

C ☐ E S S T ☐ U ☐ ☐ A M ☐ N ☐

**4** Phrase sometimes found on boxes for electronic toys:

☐ A T T ☐ R I ☐ S N O ☐ I N C ☐ U D ☐ D

**5** It might make firefighters show up for no reason:

☐ A ☐ S ☐ A L ☐ R M

**6** What the "Itsy-Bitsy Spider" went up:

☐ ☐ T E R ☐ ☐ O U T

**7** Drink made by blending fruit and ice:

S ☐ O ☐ ☐ ☐ I E

**8** Activity performed on a balance beam:

☐ Y M ☐ ☐ S ☐ I C S

**9** It will keep you warm in bed on a cold night:

E L E ☐ T ☐ ☐ ☐ B L A N ☐ ☐ ☐

**10** Outdoor meal where you might grill burgers:

☐ A R B ☐ C U ☐

20

# THE PUZZLE

Each item on the left can become an item on the right if a C is added. (For example, LANE can become LANCE.) Use a ruler to connect the dots next to the pictures that go together. Each line will cross some of the circles in the middle. The words in the untouched circles will reveal a riddle. Write each of the words *with the added Cs* in the boxes, in the order of the numbers. The highlighted boxes will spell the riddle's answer.

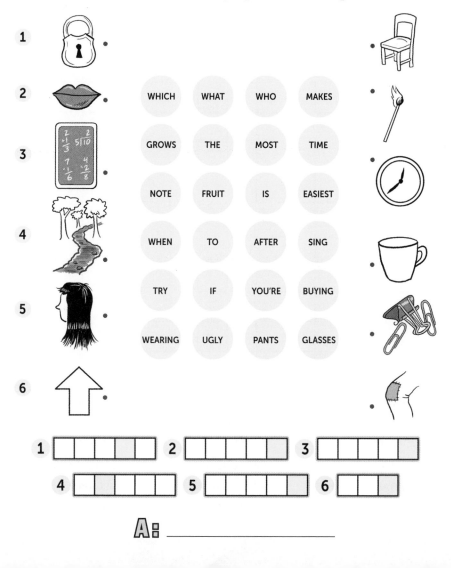

1

2

3

4

5

6

| WHICH | WHAT | WHO | MAKES |
| GROWS | THE | MOST | TIME |
| NOTE | FRUIT | IS | EASIEST |
| WHEN | TO | AFTER | SING |
| TRY | IF | YOU'RE | BUYING |
| WEARING | UGLY | PANTS | GLASSES |

1 ☐☐☐☐☐  2 ☐☐☐☐☐☐  3 ☐☐☐☐☐

4 ☐☐☐☐☐  5 ☐☐☐☐☐☐  6 ☐☐☐

A: _____

# CAP-TIVATING

The words listed below will fit into the grid like a crossword puzzle. But everywhere the letters C-A-P appear together in the words, they've been replaced in the grid with a picture of a cap. By using the numbers of letters of the words and the places where they cross as a guide, can you put them all in the correct spots? (Ignore spaces between words.) Some words may fit in different places, but there is only one way to complete the entire grid.

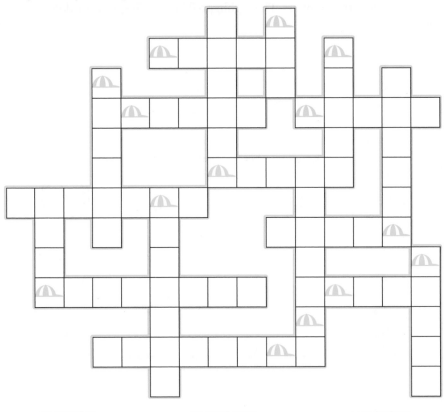

| ACAPULCO | CAPRICORN | HANDICAP |
| CAPABLE | CAPSIZE | HUBCAP |
| CAPACITY | CAPSULE | KNEECAP |
| CAPER | CAPTURE | LANDSCAPE |
| CAPITAL | DUNCE CAP | SCAPULA |
| CAPPUCCINO | FIRE ESCAPE | WHITECAPS |

# CAST PARTY

The panels in this comic strip are shown out of order. Number the blank circles with the correct order so the strip tells a funny story.

# CHICKEN AND EGG

First, connect the dots in order using a ruler to make straight lines. The path that you make will form the walls of a maze. Solve the maze by starting at the egg and finding the only path to the chicken . . . or start at the chicken and find your way to the egg.

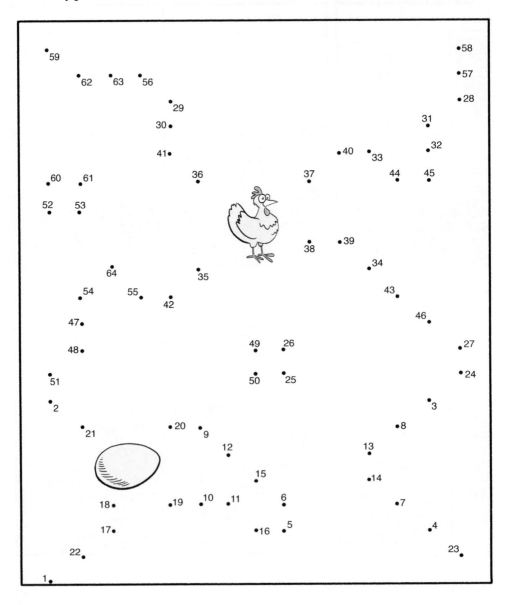

# CLOTHES CALL

Hidden in this grid, reading left, right, up, down, and diagonally are items of clothing from around the globe. When you've found them all, read the leftover letters (from left to right, top to bottom) to get a Bonus Message.

```
K  Z  E  E  M  A  K  R  A  W  L  A  H  S  F
L  I  O  N  A  T  F  A  C  R  T  H  A  F  U
E  N  M  N  S  N  S  H  B  O  L  E  R  O  Y
D  C  A  O  G  O  A  O  P  S  G  Y  R  T  F
E  U  R  U  N  D  M  O  M  E  N  I  W  E  E
R  A  E  S  O  O  N  R  U  B  O  F  Z  R  B
H  A  B  R  E  C  N  A  Y  C  R  F  L  O  A
O  D  A  S  H  I  K  I  B  T  A  E  H  E  L
S  S  Y  O  C  A  N  D  D  R  S  K  R  A  A
E  M  A  I  S  I  S  L  H  G  U  N  S  O  C
N  A  U  Y  R  E  I  N  D  O  H  T  G  T  L
N  U  G  U  R  A  D  M  A  N  T  I  L  L  A
I  S  K  A  M  H  S  A  Y  T  R  I  J  O  V
N  S  P  T  K  U  R  T  A  R  K  I  I  A  A
T  E  K  C  A  J  U  R  H  E  N  K  D  E  B
```

| | | | |
|---|---|---|---|
| BALACLAVA | DHOTI | KURTA | SARONG |
| BERET | DIRNDL | LEDERHOSEN | SERAPE |
| BOLERO | FEZ | MANTILLA | SHALWAR KAMEEZ |
| BURNOOSE | GUAYABERA | MUUMUU | SOMBRERO |
| CAFTAN | HIJAB | NEHRU JACKET | TURBAN |
| CHADOR | KEFFIYEH | PONCHO | YASHMAK |
| CHEONGSAM | KILT | RUANA | |
| DASHIKI | KIMONO | SARI | |

## BONUS MESSAGE:

_ _ _ _ _ _ _ _ _ _ _ _ _ _

_ _ _ _ _ _ _ _ _ _ _ _ _ _ _ _

_ _ _ _ _ _ _ _ _ _ :

" _ _ _ _ _ _ _ _ _ _ _ _ _ _ _ _ _ ."

25

# CODE HARD FACTS

## HOW TO SOLVE CRYPTOGRAMS

cryptogram is a message written in a code in which each letter is represented by a different letter or symbol. For example, PUZZLELOPEDIA might be represented as ✓?&&♂☞♂✗✓☞@ℙ{ or JREENLNSJLAKF.

Notice that PUZZLELOPEDIA has two Zs in a row. If you look in the same spot in the examples, you'll see two & symbols or two Es. Also, the first letter of PUZZLELOPEDIA is the same as the ninth—that's the same pattern you'll find in the cryptograms.

All writing reveals patterns like this, once you take a close look. The best way to decipher (or solve) a cryptogram is to look for patterns.

Take, for example, this coded phrase:

**AC RJ CS LCA AC RJ, AXBA NY AXJ FIJYANCL.**

At first glance, it might seem impossible to decipher. But notice those two words **AC RJ** appear twice in the phrase. Also, notice all the places **C** appears in the code—in the long word at the end, but more important, at the end of **AC**, at the beginning of **CS**, and in the middle of **LCA**. Since every English word contains at least one vowel, that **C** looks like a good candidate to be a vowel. English has only one vowel—O—that commonly appears as either the first or second letter of a two-letter word (OR, OF, TO, SO, and so on). So it's worth guessing that **C** = O. Now it looks like this:

```
  0       0      0      0                                              0
A C   R J   C S   L C A   A C   R J,   A X B A   N Y   A X J   F I J Y A N C L.
```

Next let's look at the two-letter word that ends in O. The best choices are DO, GO, NO, SO, and TO. Whatever letter you try for that **A** will show up everywhere an **A** appears. Let's try them each, one at a time:

```
D 0       0     0 D   D 0           D       D         D             D   0
A C   R J   C S   L C A   A C   R J,   A X B A   N Y   A X J   F I J Y A N C L.
```

```
G 0       0     0 G   G 0           G       G         G             G   0
A C   R J   C S   L C A   A C   R J,   A X B A   N Y   A X J   F I J Y A N C L.
```

```
N 0       0     0 N   N 0           N       N         N             N   0
A C   R J   C S   L C A   A C   R J,   A X B A   N Y   A X J   F I J Y A N C L.
```

```
S 0       0     0 S   S 0           S       S         S             S   0
A C   R J   C S   L C A   A C   R J,   A X B A   N Y   A X J   F I J Y A N C L.
```

```
T 0       0     0 T   T 0           T       T         T             T   0
A C   R J   C S   L C A   A C   R J,   A X B A   N Y   A X J   F I J Y A N C L.
```

Looking at the phrase again, you may notice the four-letter word **AXBA**, which begins and ends with the same letter. Some possibilities are DEAD, GANG, NOUN (although it can't be NOUN if the O is already assigned), SAYS, and THAT. The most common English word with this pattern is THAT, so let's give *that* a try:

```
T 0       0     0 T   T 0         T H A T         T H            T   0
A C   R J   C S   L C A   A C   R J,   A X B A   N Y   A X J   F I J Y A N C L.
```

If you read through this again, you might see another word that you can finish. That will give you a new letter to fill in throughout the phrase. And from there the rest of the message may start to look familiar. (If not, keep making educated guesses like you've been doing.)

You've just solved a cryptogram!

For another code-breaking puzzle, see List Breakers. For a fascinating story about a numerical code, see Number Crunching.

# COLOR SCHEME

To find the answer to the riddle, first use the clues to fill in the grids. The answers are the same both across and down, so enter each word in both directions. When you've filled in all the words, use the symbols to transfer those letters to the boxes below to spell the riddle's answer.

**Q** How can you paint an igloo without getting cold?

1 Part of a constellation

2 Opposite of false

3 Glow around a fairy or angel

4 "Extra! Extra! _____ all about it!"

1 Opposite of "yup"

2 So-so, but not great

3 Steady speed of a runner

4 What an optometrist checks

**A**

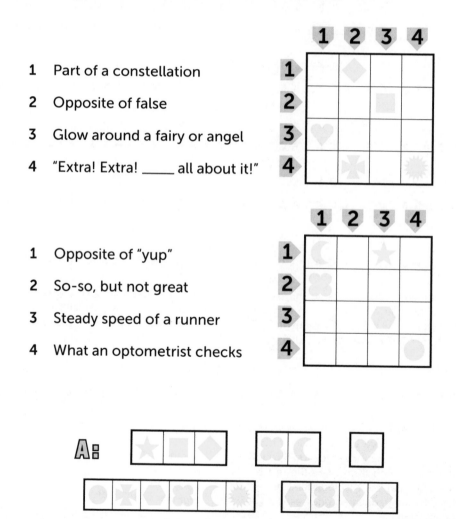

28

# CRAZY PHRAZIES

Each entry here represents a familiar phrase shown very literally. Figure out each phrase by using the placement and appearance of the words and letters as clues. For example, MOMANON is MAN IN THE MOON because the word MAN is tucked between the letters of MOON. Can you get them all?

karbeltate

BRAIN

comic

1 _____

2 _____

3 _____

INK

submarine

Quarter

4 _____

5 _____

6 _____

BJACKOX

LO HEAD HEELS VE

irighti

7 _____

8 _____

9 _____

CAKE

NETSIL

MAN
BOARD

10 _____

11 _____

12 _____

# CREEPY CRAWLIES

There are three separate spots in this swarm of bugs where a square is formed that contains one of each of the four types of bugs. Can you find all three?

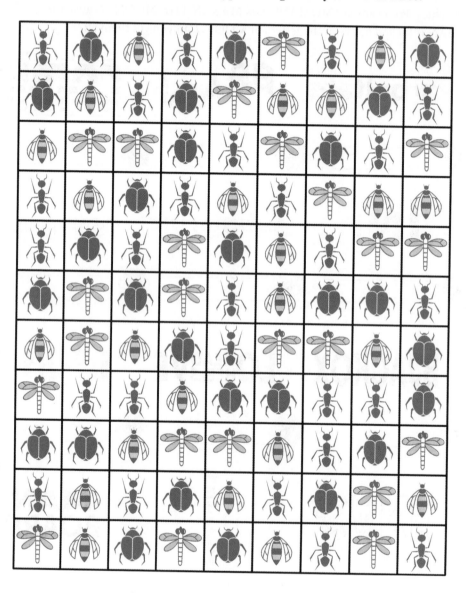

 **THE PUZZLE**

Every clue here has an answer that begins and ends with the letter D. When you've entered the answers, one column will spell a clue to an additional word that begins and ends with D. Write out the final clue and its answer at the bottom.

Shape of a baseball field

Unpaved street

Part of a car that holds the glove compartment

"You must do it!" for example

Form of transportation that uses huskies

Mickey Mouse's duck friend

You spring off this into the pool

It's wide enough for two people to sleep on

Behind schedule, like a late train or flight

Get an app onto your device

Come down the stairs

Street that has no exit

It might be shown as "$#@*&!"

"Sign on the _____ line"

**CLUE:** __ __   __ __ __ __   __   __ __ __ __ __'__-__ __ __ __.

**A:** D [ ] [ ] [ ] [ ] [ ] [ ] D

# DESERT CROSSINGS

This puzzle may make you thirsty. The desert-related words listed below will fit into the grid like a crossword puzzle. Use the lengths of the words and the places where they cross to put them in the correct spots. (Ignore spaces between words.) Some words may fit in different places, but there is only one way to complete the entire grid.

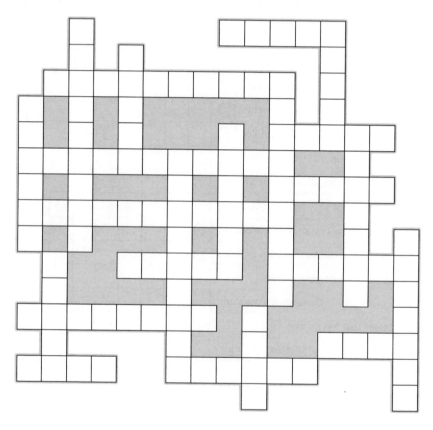

| ARMADILLOS | GILA MONSTER | MOJAVE | SANDSTORM |
| BURRO | GULCH | OASIS | SCORPION |
| CACTUS | HAWK | RATTLESNAKE | SKULL |
| CAMEL | HEAT | SAGEBRUSH | TARANTULA |
| CARAVAN | MESA | SAGUARO | YUCCA |
| DUNES | MIRAGE | SAHARA | |

# DICEDOKU

This is a 6 x 6 Sudoku puzzle that uses dice to represent numbers. Fill in each square with a different number (or side of a die) so that each number from 1 through 6 appears once in every row, column, and 3 x 2 shaded area.

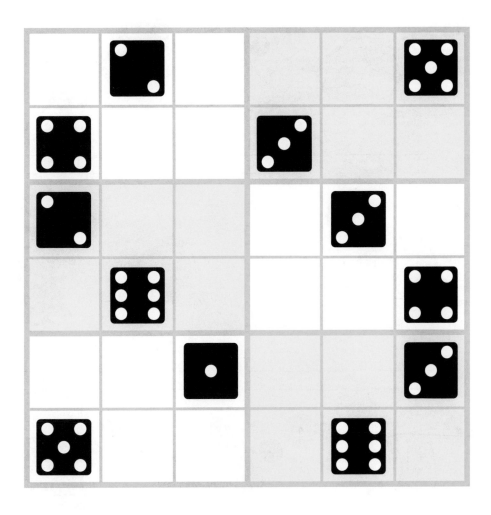

# DIDJA EVER SEE . . . ?

Maybe you've never seen a four-sided shape doing a waltz, but didja ever see a square dance? You'll need to think of familiar phrases in new and punny ways to solve this puzzle. The name of each object below, plus the name of the action shown, will form a familiar phrase. So then: Didja ever see a . . . ?

34

# DINER TALK

## SLINGING THE SLANG

**Y**ou're at a roadside diner. You order a burger, well done, with lettuce, tomato, and onion. The waitress calls out: "Hockey puck! Drag it through the garden!" Don't worry, you're not about to have the worst meal of your life. You've just heard an example of diner slang.

People who work together in the same industry often sprinkle their conversation with *jargon*, specialized words and terms that people outside the profession may not understand. You may have seen doctors on medical shows shouting "Stat!" as they rush patients to the operating room. That's short for *statim*, which means "immediately" in Latin. Real doctors and nurses understand medical jargon even if it baffles their patients.

One of the most colorful jargons of all is diner slang, which was most popular at diners and luncheonettes around the United States from the 1920s to the 1970s. Although diners are less common today, you can still hear the lingo at some old-fashioned diners.

Diner slang consists of funny phrases that the waiter or waitress shouts to the short-order cook, who understands the real meanings. Even if you have never heard these phrases before, many of them make sense, in an odd (and often unappetizing) way. A "bucket of cold mud," for example, is a bowl of chocolate ice cream. A "mouse trap" is a grilled cheese sandwich.

Here are a few more of our favorite examples:

Give it wings = serve it quickly

Two cows, make 'em cry = two burgers with onion

Moo juice = milk

Cup o' Joe = cup of coffee

Down = toast (because the bread goes down into the toaster)

Stack = order of pancakes

Cluck and grunt = eggs and bacon

Wreck 'em = scrambled eggs

---

**Can you match each example of diner slang (1–5) with its proper translation (a–e)?**

1. Dog soup
2. Cowboy with spurs
3. Let it walk
4. Nervous pudding
5. Burn the British

a. Toasted English muffin
b. Make it "to go"
c. Western omelet with French fries
d. Glass of water
e. Jell-O

# DIVIDE AND CONQUER

Divide this grid into four sections of four items, so that the items in each section have something in common. Each square must share at least one side with another square in its section, and each image can only be in one group. The common element might have to do with their names, their parts, or other connections. For example, a compass, a sewing machine, a pine tree, and a doctor all have needles. Can you identify all four groups?

# DOUBLE PLAY

We dare you to find the 12 words listed below that can follow the word *double* to make a common word or phrase. In fact, we *double* dare you, because each word is hidden in the grid *twice*! The entries read left, right, up, down, and diagonally. When you've found them all, read the leftover letters (from left to right, top to bottom) to get a Bonus Message.

```
H R E K C E D R I B B L E O A
J O I N T E D P E Y O K U E G
N J O N Y E D Y M M A H W D E
W J E O P A R D Y T D C E N N
H G T I H C I U E I S T H O T
A D O S H U B T B C N U L I E
M E M I T E B C A I K D M S N
M F N V D E L H O K B E D I A
Y D R A P O E J T U E R R V E
```

AGENT            DRIBBLE           TAKE
BED              DUTCH             TIME
CHIN             JEOPARDY          VISION
DECKER           JOINTED           WHAMMY

## BONUS MESSAGE:

\_\_\_\_\_  hit  _____  \_\_\_\_

_____  _____.

# DOUBLE SPACE

Some scientists think there might be a universe out there that's a mirror image of our own. Our astronauts haven't found it yet, but see if you can find the 28 differences in these two scenes that are *almost* mirror images of each other.

# E: THE PUZZLE

There may be a lot of variety in the spelling of the words listed below, but they all end with the sound "E." See? When you've found them all, read the leftover letters (from left to right, top to bottom) to get a Bonus Message.

```
L A E L F T E O T U T E E
T R G C H I M P A N Z E E
E S E R E G P S A D T N L
N D E I E N O E I E G L I
N E R I M E T A N R T H B
E E G E C D P S T S B O U
S K E L E T O N K E Y E J
S U D C E N U D E A E E D
E K I A R E R E B C E E D
E E I G X I R P D N A R G
W A I K I K I P K T V F Z
```

| | | | | |
|---|---|---|---|---|
| AGREE | DEGREE | GOATEE | OMG | THREE |
| BEE | EMCEE | GRAND PRIX | POTPOURRI | UNDERSEA |
| BLT | FLEA | ICED TEA | SKELETON KEY | WAIKIKI |
| CHIMPANZEE | FREE | JUBILEE | SKI | |
| DEBRIS | GLEE | KNEE | TENNESSEE | |

# BONUS MESSAGE:

\_ \_ \_ \_ \_ \_ \_ \_   \_ \_

\_ \_ \_   \_   \_ \_ \_ \_ \_   \_ \_ \_ :

\_ , \_ , \_ , \_ , \_ , \_ , \_ , \_ , \_ .

# EARTHWORM

Put the answer words into this worm, one letter in each segment. Beginning with the first word, GROUND, each new answer starts in the next numbered box and overlaps with the answer before it. For example, answer 2 starts in the box numbered 2 and begins with the letters R-O-U-N-D. Use the letters from one answer to help solve the next one, then see if you can figure out how the worm's last word connects to its first.

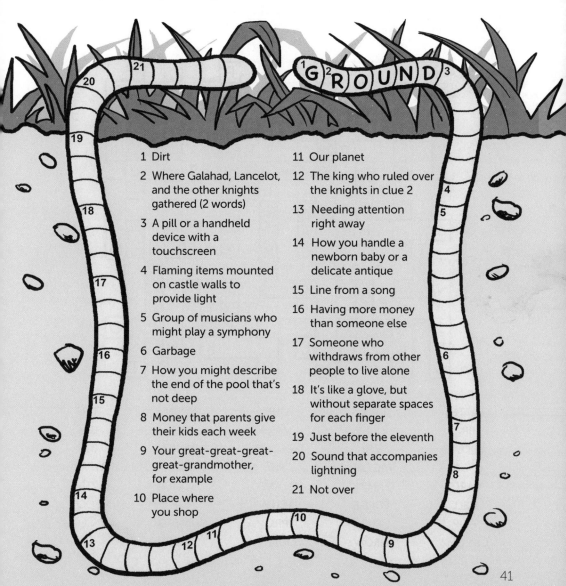

1  Dirt

2  Where Galahad, Lancelot, and the other knights gathered (2 words)

3  A pill or a handheld device with a touchscreen

4  Flaming items mounted on castle walls to provide light

5  Group of musicians who might play a symphony

6  Garbage

7  How you might describe the end of the pool that's not deep

8  Money that parents give their kids each week

9  Your great-great-great-great-grandmother, for example

10  Place where you shop

11  Our planet

12  The king who ruled over the knights in clue 2

13  Needing attention right away

14  How you handle a newborn baby or a delicate antique

15  Line from a song

16  Having more money than someone else

17  Someone who withdraws from other people to live alone

18  It's like a glove, but without separate spaces for each finger

19  Just before the eleventh

20  Sound that accompanies lightning

21  Not over

41

# ENDLESS POSSIBILITIES

The words below fit into these boxes so that they all interlock like a crossword puzzle. But each of the listed words is missing a letter at the end that will be supplied by the crossword grid to form a new word. For example, the word TUB has been placed in a spot with three boxes and a final A to form the word TUBA. By using the new endings and the lengths of the words as a guide, can you put them all in the correct spots? Careful—this one's tricky, because some words can end in more than one way. None are changed to plurals.

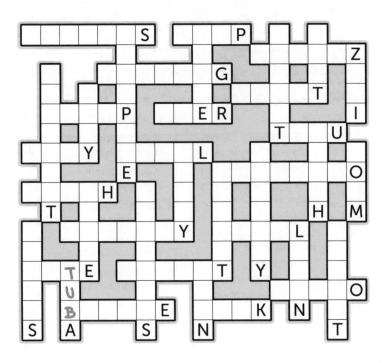

| BATTER | DISCUS | LINE | RAISIN | TENT |
| BRA | DRAW | MARS | RAN | ~~TUB~~ |
| BROWS | EAR | NEEDLES | RANG | TUT |
| BUDGE | FACTOR | PIE | RAT | WEAR |
| CARES | FLAMING | PLANE | SCAR | ZIT |
| CELL | FORGE | PLUM | SIGH | ZOO |
| COP | FUR | PRO | STAMPED | |
| DIPLOMA | GROW | QUART | TABLE | |

# ET CETERA

Each sentence contains two blanks. Fill in the first blank with a word that makes sense, and then add "et" to the end of that word to get a second word that fits in the other blank.

**1** My mom accidentally honked the _____ when she tried to swat a _____ that had landed on the steering wheel.

**2** When I grow up, I _____ to become the first astronaut to visit another _____ .

**3** Although Cinderella enjoyed dancing at the _____ , she wished that she was wearing _____ slippers instead of glass ones.

**4** The chef showed amazing _____ when it came to flipping over the crepes in that _____ .

**5** There's more money taped to the _____ behind the restaurant's cash register than I've ever had in my _____ .

**6** I took a _____ sheet of hotel stationery and wrote a note requesting a heated _____ for the bed.

**7** When the _____ began to charge toward him, the cowboy lifted his rifle and fired a single _____ into the air.

**8** You couldn't _____ a nicer day to spend outside installing a _____ fence.

**9** The astronaut who carried this _____ back to Earth traveled to the moon in a _____ .

**10** My great-grandma lived in a log _____ she built with an axe we keep in a locked _____ in the shed.

# EXTREME WORDS

## HOLDERS OF THE WORD RECORDS

Sports fans pay special attention to the fastest, the longest, the winningest. But word fans may not notice when they come across a word that holds a special place in the record books.

*Strengths*, for example, is the longest English word that has just a single vowel. And there's only one word in English that contains five vowels in a row: *queueing* (it means "lining up," and is pronounced the same as "Q-ing"). *Subcontinental* is the most common word with all five vowels in reverse alphabetical order, and *catchphrase* is the most common word containing the most consonants in a row.

The reason we specify "most common word" is that, in addition to the normal words we use every day, English also has lots of uncommon or technical words that are used only by special groups of people, like scientists. A good illustration of this is the answer to the question, "What is the longest word in the English language?"

Did you learn that the longest English word is *antidisestablishmentarianism*? There are longer words, but this one is generally regarded as the longest "real" word, with 28 letters. A longer word, the mining disease *pneumonoultramicroscopicsilicovolcanoconiosis* (with 45 letters), was actually invented by a puzzle writer in 1935 in order to create a new "longest word" for dictionaries. If you were a miner, and you had the symptoms that this disease describes, the doctor would

simply say you have *silicosis*, which has a relatively drab nine letters. That hardly seems worth it.

And what about *supercalifragilisticexpialidocious*? Sorry, but that's not a real word at all! It's a nonsense word specially created in order to have a super-long word to say. It had existed (in slightly different forms) for several decades before it was used in the movie *Mary Poppins*.

The truth is, nobody can say exactly what the longest word is or even how many words there are in English. Estimates range from 200,000 to around half a million words. You might ask, "Why don't they just count the words in the dictionary?" It's not as easy as that. For example:

*Change* is a word. *Changeable* is also a word, and so are *unchangeable* and *interchangeability*. How about the word *quasi-interchangeable*? It means "somewhat, but not completely, interchangeable." That word is not in the dictionary, but it has appeared in books and readers understand what it means. In English, adding prefixes and suffixes to words like this is allowed. Therefore, a very long word could be made this way, even if the result is a word that almost never gets used.

Speaking of *interchangeability*, that long word holds a word record of its own. Using the letters in its name, you can spell the names of a record eleven different numbers, from as low as three to as high as ninety-eight.

If you're looking for some more "Word Records," here are a few favorites:

- Longest common word with none of the five common vowels: *rhythms*.

- Longest consecutive chunk of the alphabet that appears together in any word: RSTU (this is in many words, including *overstuffed* and *understudy*).

- Many words contain all five common vowels, A, E, I, O, and U (like *sequoia*). But not many contain them in alphabetical order. The most common one is *facetiously*, which also includes the Y. (It means "not meant to be taken seriously." Seriously, that's what it means.)

- Very few words contain three consecutive double letters. Two common ones are *bookkeeping* and the hyphenated *sweet-toothed*.

- Most dotted letters in a row: *hijinks*. Also, the place names *Beijing* and *Fiji*.

- Some capital letters have "horizontal symmetry," meaning that their top half is a mirror reflection of their bottom half. (For example, H and O have this symmetry, but T doesn't.) One of the longest words to have horizontal symmetry is CHECKBOOK. If you put a mirror across the middle of this word, it will look the same.

- If you were writing out the names of all the numbers, in order, the very first letter you'd write would be Z (in *zero*). But you wouldn't write your first A until you got to *one thousand*.

- *Sleeveless* is the longest common word that has one unrepeated letter, one pair of letters, one trio of letters, and a set of four repeated letters.

The longest common "typewriter word"—that is, a word that can be spelled using only the letters in a single line on a typewriter or computer keyboard—is ten letters long. That word appears twice somewhere on this page. By looking at your own keyboard, can you figure out what it is?

# EYE EXAM

Each of the items surrounding the Cyclops has a name that can follow the word *eye* to make a familiar word or phrase. For example, if there were a picture of *drops*, the word would be *eyedrops*. Can you see your way to getting them all?

# THE PUZZLE

In each of these F-shaped grids are the letters of three items beginning with F that fit the category shown. String the letters into their words by drawing a line from box to box (moving horizontally, vertically, or diagonally in any direction). Each letter will be used only once. For an extra challenge, see if you can find all three items in each category in one unbroken line.

**NAMES OF COUNTRIES**

| A | N | F | I |
|---|---|---|---|
| L | D | J | I |
| N | F | | |
| I | E | F | |
| C | R | | |
| N | A | | |

_____

_____

_____

**KINDS OF BIRDS**

| L | C | N | F |
|---|---|---|---|
| A | O | A | L |
| F | M | | |
| O | I | N | |
| F | G | | |
| I | N | | |
| C | H | | |

_____

_____

_____

**SYNONYMS FOR "PHONY"**

| I | F | S | F |
|---|---|---|---|
| C | E | L | A |
| T | I | | |
| U | T | I | |
| S | O | | |
| A | F | | |
| K | E | | |

_____

_____

_____

**FORMS OF TRANSPORTATION**

| I | G | R | E |
|---|---|---|---|
| E | R | H | T |
| F | N | | |
| E | G | E | E |
| N | I | I | R |
| Y | F | | |
| F | R | | |
| E | R | | |

_____

_____

_____

47

# FACE VALUE

Each pair of clues on the next page will give you two three-letter words to write in the boxes. When you have an answer pair, fill in another letter in the middle to make a seven-letter word. (Below are clues for the long words but they are in *random order*.) For example, if the answers to the first pair were CAT and LOG, the seven-letter word would be CATALOG. When you're done, read down the column of single letters to complete the riddle.

**Q Why is your nose in the middle of your face?**

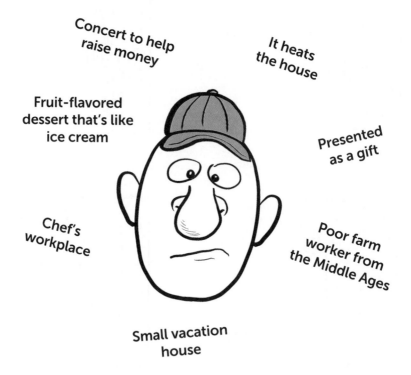

Concert to help raise money

It heats the house

Fruit-flavored dessert that's like ice cream

Presented as a gift

Chef's workplace

Poor farm worker from the Middle Ages

Small vacation house

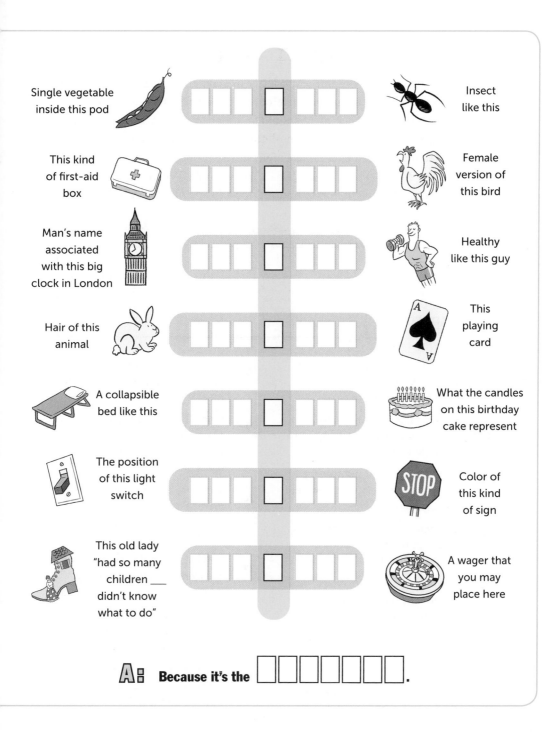

Single vegetable inside this pod

This kind of first-aid box

Man's name associated with this big clock in London

Hair of this animal

A collapsible bed like this

The position of this light switch

This old lady "had so many children ___ didn't know what to do"

Insect like this

Female version of this bird

Healthy like this guy

This playing card

What the candles on this birthday cake represent

Color of this kind of sign

A wager that you may place here

**A:** **Because it's the** ⬜⬜⬜⬜⬜⬜⬜.

49

# FAULT LINES

Each of these sentences contains a one-letter mistake that needs to be corrected. A letter might need to be added, deleted, or replaced with a new letter. (For example, in the first sentence, an M should be added to change SELL to SMELL.) First read the sentences and fix the one-letter mistakes. Then write the letter you added or deleted or used as a replacement in the proper row in the chart. The M went in the ADDED box for sentence 1, for example. When you're done, read the chart (from left to right, top to bottom) for a (somewhat) familiar message.

| | 1 | 2 | 3 | 4 | 5 | 6 | 7 | 8 | 9 | 10 | 11 | 12 | 13 |
|---|---|---|---|---|---|---|---|---|---|---|---|---|---|
| REPLACEMENT | | | | | | | | | | | | | |
| DELETED | | | | | | | | | | | | | |
| ADDED | M | | | | | | | | | | | | |

1  At our local market, if a piece of fish starts to sell, the owner will quickly lower the price.

2  I haven't been able to enjoy a breezy day ever since the spring on my kite broke.

3  After a long day of sightseeing, my family appreciated the waiter I had brought with me.

4  The detective searched the suspect's home and found a recipe for prison.

5  The new ghost was nervous because he had never hunted anybody before.

6  The doctor smiled when she told her patient that he had finally been cursed.

7  An octopus has light tentacles that help it capture its prey.

8  Until she had memorized all her lies, the actress was reluctant to meet the rest of the cast.

9  Once they found the man's fingerpaints on the wall, they knew he had committed the robbery.

10  When my friends announced they were taking me out for my birthday, it was an unexpected threat.

11  Reginald did not believe he was truly king until the clown was resting comfortably on his head.

12  The pretzels sold at the carts along the parade route were very nicely saluted.

13  The inventor thanked her patents for supporting her dreams since she was a little girl.

50

# FENCED IN

Divide this animal sanctuary into five sections so that each section is made up of five squares that touch sides and contains one of each kind of animal. The sections will not all have the same shape.

# FIGURE THAT

The answer to each clue is a phrase that contains the name of a shape. As a hint, the shape is shown in the spot where its name should appear. Can you figure them all out?

**1** Hoedown

◻ __ __ __ __ __

**2** Really disappointing

♡ __ __ __ __ __ __ __

**3** Mysterious place where many ships and planes are believed to have disappeared

__ __ __ __ __ __ __ △

**4** Honestly and without cheating

__ __ __ __  __ __ __ ◻

**5** Cold region at the top of the globe

__ __ __ __ __ __ ○

**6** Place in the White House where the president works

⬭ __ __ __ __ __ __

**7** Sports field where a pitcher's mound is located

__ __ __ __ __ __ __ __ ◇

**8** Nickname for Texas

__ __ __ __ ☆ __ __ __ __ __

**9** Place in New York City where people gather on New Year's Eve

__ __ __ __ ◻

**10** Theme song of the movie *The Lion King*

○ __ __  __ __ __ __

# FIT FOR A KING

His Royal Haughtiness wakes every day at the crack of noon and stands patiently while his courtiers get him dressed. These pictures show how he looks along the way, but they are out of order. Can you number the blank circles with the correct order so that everything is in place before he emerges on the Royal Balcony?

# FOR YOUR EYES ONLY

## HIDDEN MESSAGES

**H**ow can you write a message if you don't want everyone to see it? Use *steganography*—the art of hidden writing.

Imagine you're a general who needs to send a message to your troops. Or a celebrity who wants to arrange a meeting at a restaurant without the paparazzi knowing.

Discussing these plans openly could jeopardize them, and coded messages draw attention too. So throughout history, many surprisingly ingenious methods of sending messages have been found.

Early historians told the story of Histiaeus, an ancient Greek ruler who shaved the head of a messenger and tattooed a message on his scalp. (The messenger did not know what the message said.) Once his hair grew back, the messenger was sent to his destination with one instruction: Shave my head.

And in the 1500s, messages were written on the shells of hard-boiled eggs using invisible ink made from alum and vinegar. As the ink dried, the message disappeared from the egg's surface but seeped through the shell—and could be found *inside* on the surface of the egg white once it was peeled.

Newer methods have grown increasingly sophisticated. Take a look at the period at the end of this sentence. Small, isn't it? Now imagine that you could look at it under a microscope and see a message hidden there. This technique was developed early in the 1900s, and the periods were called *microdots*.

Digital photographs can also be used to send hidden messages. To the eye, the photograph looks normal, but some of the picture's source code (information about the colors, for example) has been replaced with a coded message. The recipient looks at the code to find the hidden information.

*Sports Illustrated* once used an old method to hide a message and fool many of its readers. In 1985, the magazine published an incredible article about Sidd Finch, a newly discovered pitcher who wore only one shoe and threw fastballs almost twice as fast as anybody else. The article began with these words: "He's a pitcher, part yogi and part recluse. Impressively liberated from our opulent life-style, Sidd's deciding about yoga . . ." The article caused a sensation until some readers noticed that the first letter of each of those words spelled "Happy April Fools' Day!"

Even a shopping list can hide a secret. The list may include completely ordinary items, but the order of the items might be important: Maybe the secret message is found by reading only the first (or last, or second) letters. A message like this is called an *acrostic*. Similarly, a message might be found by reading the first letter of each chapter in a book, or of each paragraph in an article.

Every time a message is hidden, there are specific challenges to overcome. First, the person receiving the message must be able to find and understand it. Then, the message must be incorporated smoothly. But most importantly, the item concealing the message must seem normal so it doesn't attract attention in the first place.

Keep your eyes peeled—there could be secret messages hidden all around you. Perhaps you'll even find one hidden on this page.

The name of a popular game is hidden somewhere on this page, using one of the methods described here. Can you find it?

*For some puzzles with hidden messages and words, see Bug Out, Kangagrams, Out on a Limb, Party Hopping, Re-Pair Shop, and United Nations.*

# FRANKENWORDS

Let's face it—Igor has never been known for his brains. Now he needs some help. By joining together the contents of these beakers, you can make six words associated with Halloween. Each word has a one-letter start, a three-letter middle, and a two-letter ending. Use one beaker of each size, in order from top to bottom, and stitch together your words in the spaces below.

# FROG IN THE THROAT

To find the answer to the riddle below, use the clues to fill in the words in the spaces provided. Each word is split into two halves. The arrow in each clue tells you in which direction the second half of the answer should go. When you're done, the highlighted letters, in order from top to bottom, will give the riddle's answer.

**Q:** How did the frog feel after spitting out the firefly?

| | | |
|---|---|---|
| 1 ↘ | Category for a movie that makes you laugh | |
| 2 ↗ | Really fast | |
| 2 ↘ | Phrases used by witches and wizards to make magic | |
| 3 ↗ | Impressive abilities, such as juggling or tap dancing | |
| 3 ↘ | Way of getting down the snowy slopes | |
| 4 ↗ | "G" for "General audiences" or "T" for "Teens," for example | |
| 4 ↘ | "Thanks, but I'd _____ not." | |
| 5 ↗ | Annoy | |
| 5 ↘ | Container for soda or ketchup | |
| 6 ↗ | Mild, calm, and tender | |
| 6 ↘ | Category that includes male and female | |

**A:**

# FROM END TO END

In this crossword, the answer to each clue is a word that begins and ends with the same letter, such as TWIST or COMIC. If you solve the whole thing, consider yourself a SUCCESS.

## ACROSS

1   Shape of a baseball field

4   Alternative to pants on a warm day

6   The back part

9   Slice of bread heated till it's browned

11   Circular target for an indoor game

13   "Eureka!"

14   Sound from the other side of a door

16   Admission pass

17   This ended last night at midnight

21   It should be in your lap while you're eating

22   Kind of transportation used in the Arctic

24   School exam

26   Remove pencil markings

28   Once each 365 days

30   Pleasant smell

33   It's made of panes of glass

34   The ability to sing, do magic tricks, and so on

38   A piece of gossip

39   See-through

## DOWN

1   Kind of line you might sign your name on

2   US state with the coldest temperatures

3   Father

4   Not at all meant to be funny

5   Farmer's "alarm clock"

7   Large piece of land that might include a mansion

8   Fix

10   Freshwater fish that's similar to a salmon

12   This puts juice back into batteries

15   Canoe-like boat that uses a double-ended paddle

18   Clothing size between small and large

19   Location where Lincoln gave his famous Address

20   Total and complete

23   Plant used in ancient Greece to make a wreath worn on a winner's head

25   Dasher or Dancer

26   A cyclops has one in the middle of its forehead

27   Continent whose wildlife includes zebras and giraffes

**DOWN** (continued)

**29** Scientist conked on the head by an apple

**31** Draw water up from a well

**32** Kind of dessert pastry stolen from the Queen of Hearts

**35** Continent that touches the Pacific, Indian, and Arctic Oceans

**36** Thin, sharp side of a blade

**37** Important piece of camping equipment

 **THE PUZZLE**

Each of these sentences has two blanks. Find a word for the first blank that has a pair of doubled letters. Then change those letters to GG to make a new word that fits in the second blank. For example, if the first word was SHABBY, the second would be SHAGGY.

**1** That mean kid is the _____ who pushed me out of the dune _____ I was riding.

**2** I'm _____ , but I'm not going to eat breakfast cereal after the milk has turned it all _____ .

**3** How a little baby drinks so many _____ of milk just _____ the mind.

**4** I like to _____ on the side of caution, so to make a moist cake I crack one extra _____ into my recipe.

**5** When archaeologists removed the _____ from the ancient tomb, they had to protect its wrappings from the _____ weather.

**6** I quickly _____ down your address the last time I _____ past your house.

**7** Harry Potter had to learn to _____ his voice when he didn't want a nearby _____ to hear him.

**8** Because the line always _____ while he dialed, the spy suspected that his phone was being _____ .

**9** We could hear the sailor's shirt _____ as he tried to untangle himself from the ship's complicated _____ .

**10** The barber used a _____ on the outlaw's mustache while nervously watching the man's finger on the _____ of his gun.

# "GATOR ATTACKS PUZZLE EXPERTS"

## AND OTHER STRANGE HEADLINES

The internet may have endless space, but in a printed newspaper, space is limited.

That's why newspaper headlines have come to be written in *headlinese*, in which many words are left out, shortened, or even placed out of order to save space. For example, for an article about kids and their parents criticizing school lunches, the headline might be "Kids, Parents Slam School Grub."

Headlinese may save space, but sometimes it's so hard to understand that readers get the wrong idea about what's happened. A famous example is the headline "Red Tape Holds Up New Bridge." In reality, the bridge hadn't even been built yet. "Red tape" describes complicated forms, permits, and permissions that were holding up (delaying) the new bridge's construction.

Similarly, the real headline "Gator Attacks Puzzle Experts" can be read two ways. In the correct way, experts on alligators are puzzled by a series of unexplained attacks. In the other way, a gator has attacked . . . well, people like the authors of this book.

Here are a few more actual confusing headlines. Can you figure out both the funny meaning and the intended meaning of these news stories?

1. Stolen Painting Found By Tree
2. Eye Drops Off Shelf
3. Escaped Wallaby Caught Using Huge Fishing Net
4. Shouting Match Ends Teacher's Hearing
5. Tuna Biting Off Washington Coast
6. Satellites Spot Whales from Space

*For another puzzle based on misunderstanding, see Didja Ever See . . .?*

# GEM-DANDY

In this unusual maze, begin in the triangle that says START and move to any triangle that shares a side with it. But you can only move in this sequence: WHITE – GRAY – YELLOW – WHITE – GRAY – YELLOW, and so on. Keep going until you reach the END.

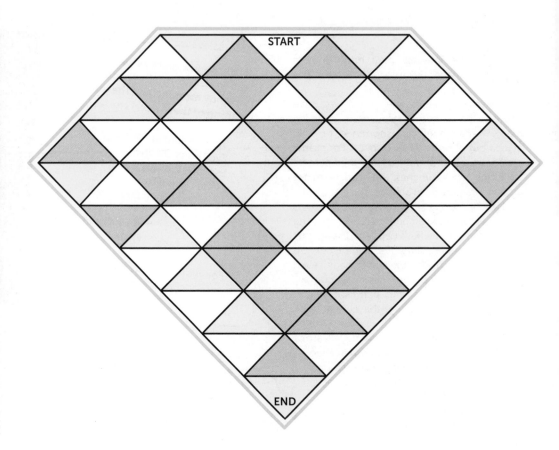

# GEO-LOGICAL

George is a very picky traveler. He recently visited Greece but not Italy, Russia but not China, and Illinois but not Wyoming. On that trip, George preferred places whose names contain double letters. In each tour below, examine the names of the places George visited and the places he skipped. Then figure out the theme and choose the spot that fits with the others. You do not need to know anything about the places to figure out what they have in common.

## ✈ TOUR 1

**GEORGE IS PLANNING TO VISIT:**

Alaska, but he'll skip Hawaii.

Casablanca but not Marrakech.

And finally Panama instead of Guatemala.

**On his way home, should he visit Havana or Santiago?**

PLACE: _____

THEME: _____

_____

## ✈ TOUR 2

**NEXT, GEORGE VISITS:**

Lincoln, Nebraska, but not Wichita, Kansas.

Jackson, Mississippi, but not New Orleans, Louisiana.

Cleveland, Ohio, but not Los Angeles, California.

**Which would he prefer: Madison, Wisconsin, or Baltimore, Maryland?**

PLACE: _____

THEME: _____

_____

## ✈ TOUR 3

**ON GEORGE'S ROUND-THE-WORLD TOUR, HE VISITED:**

Oslo but not Madrid.

Atlanta but not Chicago.

Warsaw but not Tokyo.

**Which city was on the same tour: Edinburgh or Liverpool?**

PLACE: _____

THEME: _____

_____

## ✈ TOUR 4

**ON GEORGE'S SUMMER TOUR OF THE UNITED STATES, HE LOVED:**

Dover, Delaware, but not Wilmington, Delaware.

Honolulu, Hawaii, but not Oahu, Hawaii.

Anchorage, Alaska, but not Juneau, Alaska.

**Which would he prefer to visit: Dallas, Texas, or Pittsburgh, Pennsylvania?**

PLACE: _____

THEME: _____

_____

## ✈ TOUR 5

**GEORGE'S FAVORITE TOUR INCLUDED:**

Yellowstone National Park but not Yosemite National Park.

White Plains, New York, but not Queens, New York.

Greenwich, England, but not Reykjavík, Iceland.

**Where else did he stop: Redmond, Washington, or Louisville, Kentucky?**

PLACE: _____

THEME: _____

_____

## ✈ TOUR 6

**GEORGE'S DREAM VACATION WOULD INCLUDE:**

South Korea but not Japan.

Saint Petersburg but not Moscow.

New Zealand but not Australia.

**On that same tour, would he stop in Buenos Aires or Lima?**

PLACE: _____

THEME: _____

_____

# GOING GREEN

Ready to think global? Hidden in this grid are words and phrases about the environment. When you've found them all, read the leftover letters (from left to right, top to bottom) to get a Bonus Message.

```
T  N  I  R  P  T  O  O  F  N  O  B  R  A  C
N  I  L  N  T  X  H  O  R  G  A  N  I  C  E
E  F  I  U  Y  C  N  E  G  R  U  T  U  N  R
M  E  F  G  R  E  Y  A  L  E  N  O  Z  O  S
N  S  E  V  R  E  S  N  O  C  C  H  H  H  O
O  N  M  R  E  U  S  A  B  L  E  Y  A  I  L
R  B  I  O  D  E  G  R  A  D  A  B  L  E  A
I  C  L  D  G  R  R  E  L  E  I  R  N  T  R
V  P  L  A  N  E  T  E  W  T  L  I  O  S  P
N  M  A  E  C  Y  A  R  A  S  O  D  K  A  O
E  W  E  Y  A  D  H  T  R  A  E  C  H  W  W
Y  R  C  I  D  N  I  W  M  S  T  A  E  A  E
G  L  P  O  L  L  U  T  I  O  N  R  T  A  R
E  T  A  M  I  L  C  H  N  E  S  E  K  Y  N
B  R  O  E  N  D  A  N  G  E  R  E  D  W  N
```

| | | | |
|---|---|---|---|
| BINS | ENVIRONMENT | OXYGEN | SOLAR POWER |
| BIODEGRADABLE | GLOBAL WARMING | OZONE LAYER | TREE |
| CARBON FOOTPRINT | GREEN | PLANET | URGENCY |
| CLEAN | HABITAT | POLLUTION | WASTE |
| CLIMATE | HYBRID CAR | RECYCLE | WATER |
| CONSERVE | LIFE | REUSABLE | WIND |
| EARTH DAY | OCEAN | SMOG | |
| ENDANGERED | ORGANIC | SOIL | |

## BONUS MESSAGE:

___ ___ ___ ___ ___   ___ ___ ___ ___ ___ ___ ___ ,

___ ___ ___ ___ ___ ___ ___ ___ ___ ___   ___ ___ ___ ___

" ___ ___ ___ ___ ___ ___ ___ ___   ___ ___ ___ ___ ___ ?"

64

# GOODNIGHT MOO

To find the answer to the riddle, name the pictures shown here. Then fit those words into the boxes below. Each word is a different length, so there is only one way to place each answer. When you're done, the circled letters, in order, will reveal the riddle's answer.

**Q:** Why should you go to sleep when the cows go to sleep?

**A:** _____ .

# GRADE EXPECTATIONS

The panels in this comic strip are shown out of order. Number the blank circles with the correct order so the strip tells a funny story.

# GRAVEYARD SHIFT

Stay very alert or you might get lost in this graveyard. Start by examining everything about the tombstone in the upper left corner—the stone's shape, the image carved onto it, and the items lurking there. Now find an *exact duplicate* of one of those elements (shape, image, or item) at any other grave on the page and float over to it. Then choose a different element from *that* new grave and find its duplicate somewhere else. Keep going until you arrive at the grave at the bottom right. Beware: There are lots of dead ends, but only the one marked DEAD END is your final resting place!

# GRIDLOCK

In these mini crosswords, the answers to all the clues have the same number of letters: three in the top grids, and four in the bottom. Clues are given for all the words, but they are in random order. There is only one way to fit the words into each grid so that half the words read across and the other half read down. Can you fill all the grids? Some letters have been placed to help you get started.

## PUZZLE 1

Attempt

Had a meal

Hurricane's center

Not wet

Opposite of subtract

Stuff for coloring fabric or Easter eggs

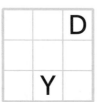

## PUZZLE 2

Drink that's served hot or iced

Insect that lives in a hill

It flies out of a cave

Large vase

Period of time

Place to take a bath

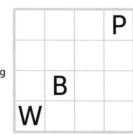

## PUZZLE 3

Bump on a witch's chin

Cooking appliance

Departed or left

Enthusiastic five-star review

Get larger

Molten rock flowing from a volcano

Not under

Shine in the dark like a firefly

## PUZZLE 4

Equipment for a gardener or firefighter

Having the skill to do something

Loose item of clothing worn after a bath

Melt or become unfrozen

Secretly take a look

Seven days

Small piece of land surrounded by water

Vacation or journey

# GUESS LIST

Fill in each of the miniature crosswords on this page with the complete set of words that make up the category—but it's up to you to supply those words. One letter in each puzzle has been placed to get you started. Use the lengths of words and the letters where they cross to help you fill in every word in each set.

MONTHS

SENSES

CHESS PIECES

GREAT LAKES

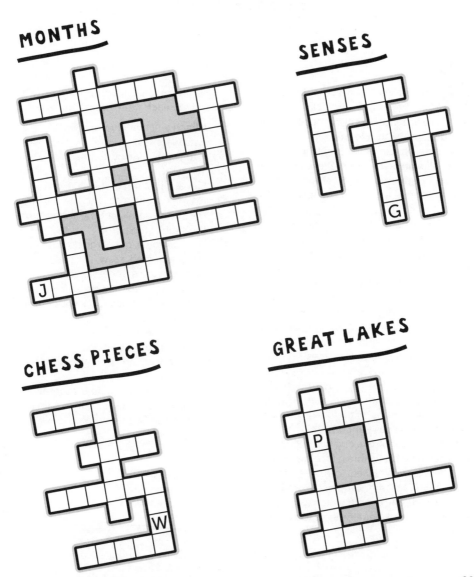

# GUY GARGOYLE, GIRL GARGOYLE

## TING TWUSTERS

Can you say "An old reliable tea kettle" five times fast? No problem. How about "A proper copper coffeepot"? That's probably a lot harder.

The first phrase rolls smoothly off the tongue, allowing you to move easily from one sound to the next. Say it slowly and feel how your tongue and lips move around. The second phrase is likely to make you stop and think: What's the next sound? How do I get there from where I am now? You might wind up saying "A proper coffer copy cot" or something similar. You've just twisted your tongue.

Tongue twisters exist in every language. In Cantonese, the phrase "Enter the laboratory and press the emergency button" sounds like this: *Yap sat yim sat gam gan gap jai.* In Spanish (where tongue twisters are called *trabalenguas*, or "tongue obstacles"), *A mí me mima mi mamá* means "My mother spoils me" and *Pancha plancha con cuatro planchas. ¿Con cuantas planchas plancha Pancha?* means "Pancha irons with four irons. With how many irons does Pancha iron?"

Tongue twisters are taxing for tongues but, it turns out, hard on the brain too. In an experiment, people were asked to read sentences silently. Some of the sentences contained tongue twisters and others, which were just as long, did not. The tongue twisters took longer to read.

Here are some favorite tongue twisters. Try and say each three times fast. Good luck!

- Which wristwatches are Swiss wristwatches?
- Red leather, yellow leather
- Toy boat
- Sieves sift a fifth of thistles.
- A skunk sat on a stump. The skunk thunk the stump stunk, but the stump thunk the skunk stunk.
- Guy gargoyle, girl gargoyle
- Mr. See owned a saw.
  And Mr. Soar owned a seesaw.
  Now, See's saw sawed Soar's seesaw before Soar saw See, which made Soar sore.
  Had Soar seen See's saw before See sawed Soar's seesaw,
  See's saw would not have sawed Soar's seesaw.
  So See's saw sawed Soar's seesaw.
  But it was sad to see Soar so sore just because See's saw sawed Soar's seesaw.

In what language are tongue twisters known as "finger fumblers"?

 **THE PUZZLE**

Follow the eight instructions below. Each will lead you to cross out one or more words in the grid, so look carefully to make sure you've got them all. When you're done, there will be two words remaining. Together, these words spell something you may find in a bathroom. But if you remove the H, they spell something you may find in a living room.

**1** Cross out any word that becomes a new word with the same pronunciation if H is added to the beginning.

**2** Cross out any word that can become a new word if the H is moved from somewhere else in the word to the beginning.

**3** Cross out any word that will spell the name of a number if an H is deleted.

**4** Cross out any word that will spell the name of a number if an H is inserted.

**5** Cross out any word that can become a word for a family member if the H is deleted.

**6** Cross out any word that, when you add an H at the beginning, becomes a new word that describes the action of the original word.

**7** Cross out any word that becomes the name of a living thing if the second letter is changed to H.

**8** Cross out any word that becomes a new word if the last letter is changed to H.

| | | |
|---|---|---|
| **HEIGHT** | | **EAR** |
| **OURS** | | **PLEASANT** |
| **HAIR** | **SPARK** | **THEN** |
| **TREE** | **HAUNT** | **FORTY** |
| **SCRIMP** | **CONDITIONER** | **STEEP** |
| **RICE** | | **EARTH** |

 _____ _____ → _____ _____

(BATHROOM)          (LIVING ROOM)

71

# HARDY HAR HAR

Don't be fooled! Only one of these silhouettes matches the picture in the center. Can you tell which, and spot the differences in the others?

# HAVING IT BOTH WAYS

Fill in the grids with the letters shown so that each grid contains two words that are opposites. The letter where the two words cross has been placed. For example, the first one is COME and GO, crossing at the O. Can you get them all?

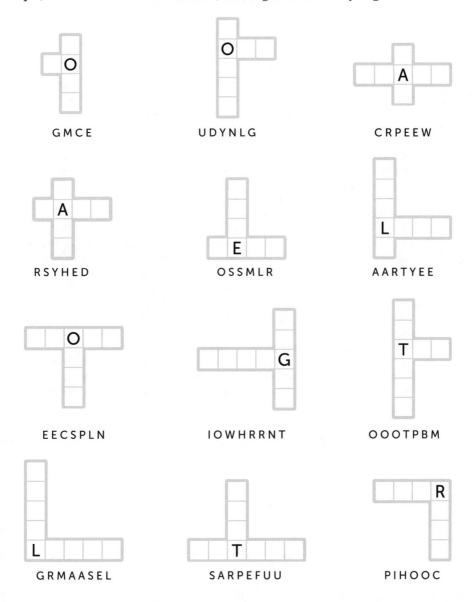

GMCE

UDYNLG

CRPEEW

RSYHED

OSSMLR

AARTYEE

EECSPLN

IOWHRRNT

OOOTPBM

GRMAASEL

SARPEFUU

PIHOOC

# HERE'S THE POOP . . .

## ON PALINDROMES

A *palindrome* is a word or message that says the same thing when it's read forward or backward. Some common palindromes are MOM and DAD, as well as longer ones like KAYAK and LEVEL. In these palindromes, the word's letters are in the same order in either direction.

Phrases or even complete sentences can also be palindromes. In these cases, reading the palindrome backward usually requires the reader to shift the spacing and punctuation. For example, while the letters in the phrase "Never odd or even" are the same in either direction, the true spacing in reverse would read "Neve ro ddo reven." The same is true of the question "Borrow or rob?" The punctuation and the spaces between words have to be ignored to read it in reverse.

In "Don't nod," the apostrophe simply jumps into the space on the other side of the T. In "pull-up," the hyphen moves to the other side of the two Ls.

People have spent many hours coming up with sentence-long palindromes. Some favorites are: "Was it a rat I saw?," "Yo, Banana Boy!," and "Ma is as selfless as I am." The longer the sentence, unfortunately, the less sense it usually makes. An example is something a fish eater might say to his doctor: "Doc, note—I dissent. A fast never prevents a fatness. I diet on cod."

Other palindromes use complete *words* as their smallest unit. That is, you can read each word as a unit from left to right or from right to left, and the sentence will be the same. One favorite is "You can cage a swallow, can't you . . . but you can't swallow a cage, can you?," which was written by James A. Lindon, a writer of many clever language tricks. Betsy Mirarchi wrote this description of autumn's end: "Fall leaves after leaves fall."

You can try writing a palindromic sentence, but be warned: If you get stuck, you'll have to go right back to the beginning.

TWO WAYS

The motto of the Three Musketeers contains seven words that appear in the same order in both directions. What's that motto?

*For words that spell a different word in reverse (such as WARTS and STRAW), see Zeus Returns to Suez: A Look Back at Reversals.*

# HIT OR MISS

This may look like a mega game of tic-tac-toe, but it's actually a kind of logic puzzle. The object is to fill the blank spaces in each grid so that there are never more than three Xs or Os in a row—not across, not down, and not diagonally. Hint: If you find three in a row of one kind, you know that you can put the other kind into the spaces on either end.

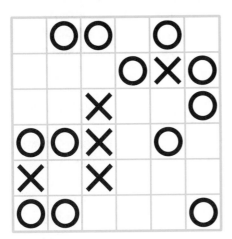
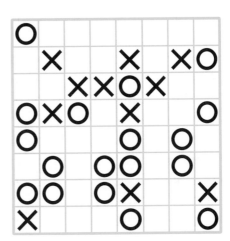

# HOLED-UP NOTE

A bear put out this sign before hibernating. But you can rearrange the letters to make a new sign that would still work. Scrambling each word separately, what would the new sign say?

QUITE ASLEEP

# HOT STUFF

Here's a hot topic: This grid contains the names of things that are hot. When you've found them all, read the leftover letters (from left to right, top to bottom) to get a Bonus Message.

```
L I G P H S P O T L I G H T A
T C F U H N I N A G I S F V I
R A P O T P A L U F T Y A T H
E R W S N O R I G N I L R U C
Y E O U S D S A U N B E A C H
R N R E N R U B S D D M E G I
D G R E E S E T F A A H S Z
R I R B E N G R I D D L E C Z
I N M S H O D E O I T F O I U
A E R T L S E O W T H S I P C
H T A E R B S N O G A R D O A
C C L R H I E S O U M I F R J
U U R N C H R H N V O F D T T
Y T U O E R T A T H E A N A T
H S E S T O A S T E R N U N R
```

AUGUST
BEACH
BURNER
CAR ENGINE
COFFEE
CURLING IRON
DESERT
DRAGON'S BREATH
EMBERS
FLAME
FONDUE
GRIDDLE
HAIR DRYER
JACUZZI
LAPTOP
LAVA
OVEN
RADIATOR
SAUNA
SHOWER
SOUP
SPOTLIGHT
STERNO
SUN
TOASTER
TORCH
TROPICS
YULE LOG

## BONUS MESSAGE:

_ _ _ _ _ _ _ _ _ _ _ _

_ _   _ _ _ _ _ _

_ _ _ _ _ _ _ _ _ _ _ _

_ _ _ _ _ _ _ _ _ _

_ _ _ _ _ _ _ _ _ _ _ _ _

_ _   _ _ ,

_ _ _ _ _ _ _ _ _ _

_ _ _ _ _ _ _ _ _ _ _

_ _ _ _ _ _ _ _ _ _ _ _ _ .

# THE PUZZLE

In this game of I Spy, there are 20 things in the picture that end with the letter I. Can you eye them all?

# ICE PACK

The things listed below will fit into these boxes so the words all interlock like a crossword puzzle. But when the letters I-C-E appear together in a word, they have been replaced in the grid with a picture of an ice cube. By using the lengths of the words and the places where they cross as a guide, can you put them all in the correct spots? Some words may fit in different places, but there is only one way to complete the entire grid.

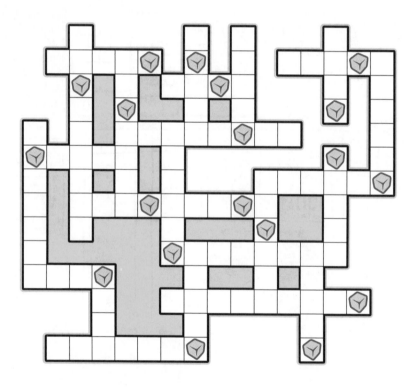

| ADVICE | ICE SKATERS | POLICE OFFICER | SOLSTICE |
| CHOICES | LICENSE | PRACTICE | SUFFICE |
| CREVICE | LICORICE | PRECIPICE | TRICERATOPS |
| ICE AGE | MALEFICENT | PRICE TAG | UNICEF |
| ICE CAPS | NOTICE | REJOICE | VICE VERSA |
| ICED TEA | ORANGE JUICE | SERVICE | VOICEMAIL |

# INCREDIBLE EDIBLES

Describe each of these scenes with two similar words in which the first word is a food and the second word is the same except for one changed letter. For example, a bowl of steaming broth with a lather-covered floating bar would illustrate SOUP SOAP. Can you figure out the names of all eight pictures?

1  _ _ _ _
   _ _ _ _

2  _ _ _ _ _
   _ _ _ _ _

3  _ _ _ _ _
   _ _ _ _ _

4  _ _ _ _ _
   _ _ _ _ _

5  _ _ _ _
   _ _ _ _

6  _ _ _ _ _ _
   _ _ _ _ _ _

7  _ _ _ _ _ _
   _ _ _ _ _ _

8  _ _ _ _ _ _ _
   _ _ _ _ _ _ _

# ISLAND TOUR

See if you can find your way through this beach maze by moving left, right, up, or down (but not diagonally) to the next picture only if it is either the same color (black, gray, or yellow) or the same object as the one you're on. Start on the black sand dollar at the upper left corner. From there, you may move either to the black starfish next to it or to the gray sand dollar below it. Keep moving until you reach the yellow seashell in the bottom right corner.

**START**

**FINISH**

# IS THAT A FACT?

Even the smartest people are surprised by facts once in a while. First think carefully about each question, then take a guess at the answer. In some cases it's completely obvious . . . but in other cases it's completely unexpected. This quiz is most fun if you learn each answer before you move on to the next question, so you might want to have someone else verify each answer as you solve. Get ready to guess and "guess again"!

**1** True or false? The formula for Coca-Cola is not patented.

**2** When Albert Einstein was a schoolboy, how were his grades in math?

☐ Excellent

☐ Poor

**3** What is the opposite of *inflammable*?

**4** What is paper money made of?

**5** In the book *20,000 Leagues Under the Sea*, what is the deepest that the submarine *Nautilus* goes?

☐ Less than 20,000 leagues

☐ Exactly 20,000 leagues

☐ More than 20,000 leagues

**6** You and your friend pick six numbers between 1 and 75 for a lottery. Your friend chooses 8, 11, 24, 28, 56, 63. You choose 1, 2, 3, 4, 5, 6. Whose set of numbers has a better chance of coming up in a random drawing?

**7** Why would you get in trouble for trying to sell octopus bones?

**8** True or false? Woodrow Wilson, who was president during all of World War I, never said or wrote the term "World War I," and none of his staff used that term during the war either.

**9** Which has more bones in its neck—a giraffe or a human?

**10** In which two directions does an elevator travel?

**11** What animal were the Canary Islands named for?

**12** If a sound is produced at the end of a solid iron rod that's one mile long, and the same sound is simultaneously produced at the end of a hollow cardboard tube the same length, which sound arrives at the other end first?

☐ The sound through the iron rod

☐ The sound through the hollow tube

☐ Neither—they arrive at the same time

# IT ALL ADDS UP

## MAGIC SQUARES

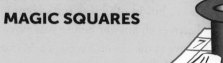

**A**magic square is a square grid where consecutive numbers are placed so that the digits across each row, down each column, and even along both long diagonals add up to the same number. That sum is the magic number. Here's a 3 × 3 magic square, using all the numbers 1 through 9:

| 4 | 9 | 2 |
|---|---|---|
| 3 | 5 | 7 |
| 8 | 1 | 6 |

The three numbers in every row, column, and diagonal add up to the magic number 15.

Thousands of years ago, magic squares were thought to actually be magical. A Chinese legend describes a magic square called the Lo Shu square. In ancient times, the Lo River flooded, causing great destruction. Sacrifices were offered to calm the angry river god, but nothing improved—until a child noticed that a turtle that came from the river and walked around the sacrifices had interesting markings on its shell. Each section, which formed a 3 × 3 square, had a different number of dots. It was, in fact, the magic square shown above, with dots instead of numbers. The people understood that the magic number was 15, and they could finally make the river god happy with the correct number of sacrifices: 15.

In 2014, a region in China called Macau introduced a special set of stamps featuring nine different magic squares. The values of the stamps are 1 through 9 *patacas* (the local currency)—and the arrangement of the stamps on the printed sheet forms a Lo Shu square. Well played, Macau postal service.

Here is a 4 × 4 magic square that uses the numbers 1 through 16 and appears on one of the stamps from Macau. But some of the numbers are missing here. The magic number that each row, column, and long diagonal adds up to is 34. Using both math and logic, can you figure out what numbers belong in the empty spaces? Tip: List all the numbers from 1 to 16, and cross each off once it has been placed.

| 16 |   |   | 13 |
|----|---|---|----|
|    |   |   | 8  |
|    | 6 | 7 |    |
| 4  |   | 16 |   |

# IT'S NO USE!

Each object here is missing something important that would make it difficult, if not impossible, to use properly. Take a good look and see if you can spot what isn't there.

 **THE PUZZLE**

There are lots of familiar pairs where the second item starts with J, like "flotsam and jetsam." Draw a straight line from each word on the left to its J partner on the right. (Use the points of the arrows as the ends of your lines.) This will cross out some of the circled letters in the middle. When you're finished, read the leftover letters from top to bottom to get one more item that goes with J.

| JACK | | JULIET |
| PRIDE | V        N | JOY |
| | I | |
| BEN | X    P    L | JANE |
| | A    T    E | |
| ROMEO | | JILL |
| | R    K    B | |
| TARZAN | O | JURY |
| | S | |
| JUDGE | | JERRY |

**A:** _____

# JAM SESSIONS

Write the answer to each clue in the boxes above or below it. The words overlap, so every word you fill in will help you get the words next to it.

**1**

| yellow fruits with peels | book misspelling | very important! | allowed by law | like Rapunzel's hair |
|---|---|---|---|---|

| rude and mean | rain hard | safe and tame | four quarts |
|---|---|---|---|

**2**

| sense with your tongue | too | opposite of vanish | last but not ____ | mistake |
|---|---|---|---|---|

| rob | bath item | surprise in an oyster | egg-dyeing holiday |
|---|---|---|---|

**3**

| sport where you ride waves | item on a to-do list | a bad sign | small stones on a path |
|---|---|---|---|

| part of your hand | not in any special order | carve words into metal |
|---|---|---|

**4**

| did things hurriedly | two-faced zodiac sign | wrapped-up body | express gratitude | jump far |
|---|---|---|---|---|

| wall of shrubs | the smallest amount | ancient legend | part of the foot |
|---|---|---|---|

85

# JEWEL BOX

Move just one jewel from one compartment to another so that each row has the same number of jewels and both columns also have the same number of jewels.

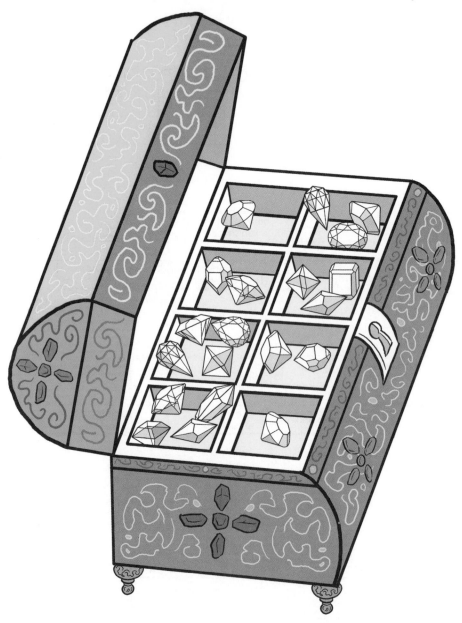

# JOB OPENINGS

Each line represents the name of an occupation. Some letters have been replaced by pictures shaped like those letters, which will provide visual clues. Fill in one letter per blank to get the names of the occupations. Can you get them all?

# JUMPING THROUGH HOOPS

## WRITING WITH RIDICULOUS RESTRICTIONS

**W**riting is hard work, but some writers actually enjoy coming up with difficult rules, or *constraints*, to make writing even harder. Poets have composed works in which every line starts with the next letter of the alphabet or in which every word is one letter longer than the last. In the novel *Alphabetical Africa*, author Walter Abish wrote all of Chapter 1 using only words beginning with A; Chapter 2 used only words beginning with A or B; and so on until Chapter 26, when any letter was allowed. Then he dropped one letter in each of the next 26 chapters until the last chapter, when he again used only words starting with A.

One of the greatest constrained writing accomplishments of all time was a book by French writer Georges Perec (who also wrote crossword puzzles) called *La Disparition* (The Disappearance). What makes it special is that the letter E does not appear anywhere in the entire 300-page book—not even in the title. (However, Perec couldn't avoid including four Es on the cover: They're in his name!) Keep in mind that E is the most common letter used in French, just as it is in English.

Amazingly, Perec's book has been translated into languages around the world. Each time, the translator has retold Perec's original story while leaving out the most common letter in the translator's own language. For example, in English, it is titled *A Void*, and once again, there are no Es.

In 1960, a publisher bet a famous writer that he could not write a children's book using only 50 different words. Not only did that author succeed, but today that book is one of the most popular children's books of all time.

Do you know what book this is? Hint: Four of the 50 words are *fox*, *train*, *box*, and *like*.

 ## THE PUZZLE

Somewhere in this tangle of lines is the outline of a capital letter K that looks like this: **K**. There may be other lines inside the K, but there will be only one spot with a set of lines that works. The K might be rotated in any direction. Can you find it?

# KANGAGRAMS

A *kangagram* is a word that contains all the letters of a shorter word, in order, that means the same thing as the longer word. For example, INSTRUCTOR is a kangagram containing the shorter word TUTOR. Each entry here shows the letters of the shorter word. Fill in the blanks to get the longer word. How many can you get?

1   B U __ S T

2   M A R __ __ T

3   B L O __ __ O M

4   __ H __ __ __ E N

5   F R A __ I L __

6   __ E A __ T

7   C __ O C O __ A __ __

8   M __ __ E __ __

9   __ __ __ __ __ U R __ G E

10   D E __ __ A __ __ D

11   __ V A C __ A T E

12   __ S T __ U N __

13   M A __ __ __ L __ __ E

90

# KEEPING YOUR WORD

For each set of four words, think of a single word that can follow each one of them to get four familiar phrases. Write that word in the dotted box. For example, the words SLED, HOT, GUIDE, and POLICE can all be followed by DOG. Each set has a different word as its answer. When you've gotten all five answer words, look at them as a new set—those words *also* have a single word that can follow them. Can you get them all?

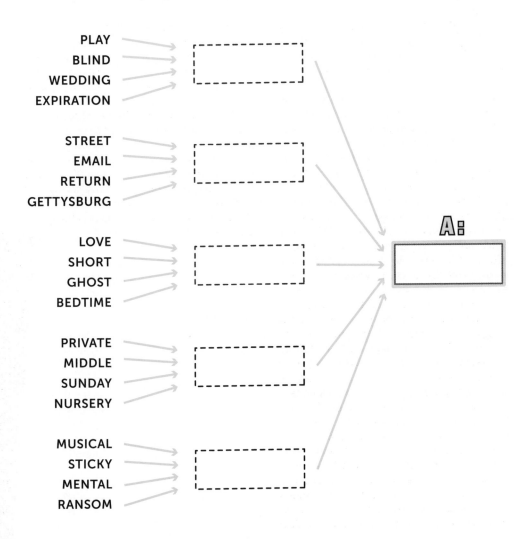

PLAY
BLIND
WEDDING
EXPIRATION

STREET
EMAIL
RETURN
GETTYSBURG

LOVE
SHORT
GHOST
BEDTIME

PRIVATE
MIDDLE
SUNDAY
NURSERY

MUSICAL
STICKY
MENTAL
RANSOM

A:

TOP SECRET

# KEY WORDS

## THE SECRET HISTORY OF CROSSWORDS IN WWII

When Britain was battling Germany during World War II, the British government needed people who were good at cracking codes to help win the war. They contacted mathematicians and *linguists* (language specialists), but they also decided to find people who were good at solving "cryptic crosswords"—what the British call their crossword puzzles.

They did it by asking the *Daily Telegraph*, a British newspaper, to organize a crossword contest, with a prize given to anyone who could solve the puzzle in less than 12 minutes. The winning contestants later received an envelope marked CONFIDENTIAL with a letter asking them for their help on a secret project. Those people joined a large group who eventually cracked Germany's toughest codes. This was important work that remained secret for more than 30 years.

But that's not the only time that the *Daily Telegraph*'s puzzles caught the attention of the British government. In 1944 British, American, and Canadian forces spent months planning a massive, top-secret mission, which was given the code name Operation Overlord. Only a very small group of people knew all the details, such as locations and the exact day the mission would take place. It was so secret that many of the most important details were replaced with code words.

But as the invasion day grew closer, a curious thing began to happen. A number of those code words began to appear as answers in the *Telegraph* crosswords. Just two weeks before the mission, the code word *Omaha* (used for one of the attack locations) showed up in a puzzle. Later that week, the word *Overlord* itself appeared! All told, about ten of the code words were used in the days leading up to the invasion.

All of the crosswords were written by one man, Leonard Dawe, who was headmaster (or principal) of a boys' school. The British security agency became alarmed that Dawe might be using his puzzles to send secret signals to the enemy. Investigators actually showed up at Dawe's home for intensive questioning. Eventually they decided he was innocent, and they let him go.

One of the following choices explains what happened, but the other two are fakes. Which one is the real ending to the story?

a. The head of British intelligence had secretly told Dawe to include the words in order to confuse the enemy, in case they had learned about the secret mission but didn't know when it would take place.

b. The words were suggested by Dawe's students, who heard them spoken by soldiers stationed near the school.

c. It turns out that Dawe was a spy after all; he disappeared after the war ended, and nobody has seen or heard from him since 1946.

# KNIGHT WATCH

Only two of these confused knights are exactly alike. Can you tell which, and spot the differences in the others?

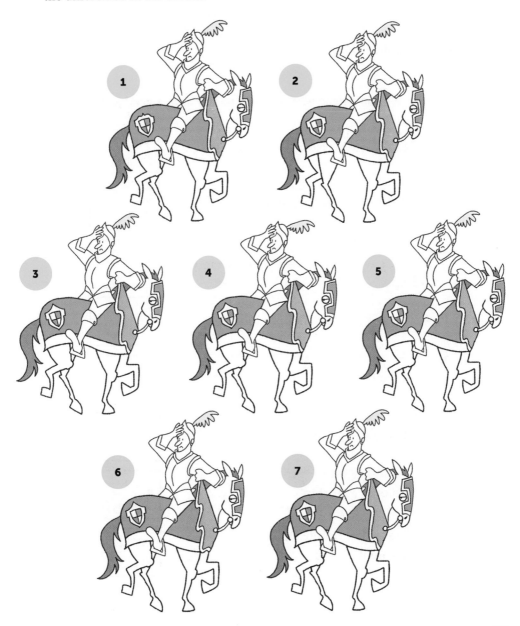

# KNOTTY SITUATIONS

The answer to each clue is a seven-letter word that starts and ends with the same letter. That letter is given, so start your answer word there, go around the grid in the direction of the arrow, and end on the letter where you began. (The first answer, CHAOTIC, is filled in to show you how it works.) When you're done, the middle column will spell the answer to the riddle.

**Q** Why do people who tie knots all day have a good job?

1. Completely disorganized

2. Running behind schedule

3. State whose capital is Montgomery

4. People who do "figure eights"

5. Italian herb often used on pizza

6. Sorrow

7. Male TV reporter

8. Snake that noisily shakes its tail before it strikes

**A** _ _ _ _   _ _ _ _   _ _ _ _   _ _ _ _.

# KOOKY CUTTERS

At Hairbrains Hair Salon, these six stylists do each other's hair for free. Whenever somebody needs a cut, they choose one of the stylists with just the right skills. It all works out so that every stylist gets one haircut and every stylist gives one haircut. Can you figure out who cuts whose hair? *Note: There is no pair of stylists who just cut each other's hair.*

HELLO
MY NAME IS
**AL**
BEST AT SHAVING HEADS

HELLO
MY NAME IS
**BRITTANY**
BEST AT HANDLING
CURLY HAIR

HELLO
MY NAME IS
**CARL**
GREAT WITH LONG HAIR

HELLO
MY NAME IS
**DAVE**
BEST WITH WOMEN'S
HAIRSTYLES

HELLO
MY NAME IS
**EHSAN**
EXCELLENT AT
BEARD TRIMMING

HELLO
MY NAME IS
**FRAN**
VERY GOOD AT
TRIMMING MUSTACHES

AL cuts _____'s hair.

BRITTANY cuts _____'s hair.

CARL cuts _____'s hair.

DAVE cuts _____'s hair.

EHSAN cuts _____'s hair.

FRAN cuts _____'s hair.

# THE PUZZLE

The answer to every clue here is a word that contains double Ls. First read the clues and fill in all the words. When you're done, read down the highlighted columns to complete the answer to the riddle.

**Q:** Why did the stressed-out cat need two Ls?

1  Structures you see in the Dutch countryside

2  Bird often found at the beach

3  Inflatable party decoration

4  "Good-bye! So long! Take care!"

5  Shakespeare's first name

6  Low area between two hills

7  Hard candy on a stick

8  A dictionary breaks words into these pieces

9  Money your parents give you every week

10  Tree that's described as "weeping"

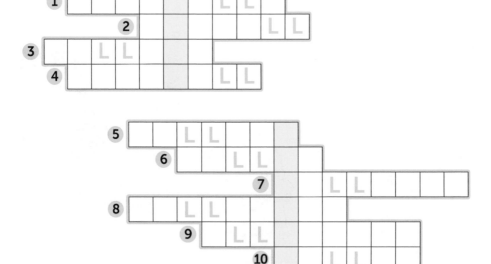

**A:** To make his ___ ___ ___  ___ ___ ___ ___ ___

96

# LAST WORD

It's always nice to get the last word. Think you can get it here? Find and cross out the words at the bottom that match the instructions, till only one word is left.

**1** This word contains three sets of double letters in a row.

**2** The names of all the letters in this word rhyme with each other.

**3** If you remove the first letter of this word, or the first two letters, or the first three letters, the remaining letters will still spell a word.

**4** If you add a letter to the start of this word, you can spell a word with the opposite meaning of the original word.

**5** This word can become a boy's name if you change the last letter to K and a girl's name if you change the last letter to Y.

**6** If you remove the first and last letters of this word, the remaining letters will spell the name of a food.

**7** If you read this word backward, it spells a different word.

**8** If you rearrange the letters in each of these two words, you can spell two compass directions.

**9** Move the second letter of this word to the end to get a string of letters that are all next to each other in the alphabet.

**10** Delete the first four letters of this word and the remaining letters will spell a type of weapon.

**11** If you remove the last letter of this three-syllable word, it will become a one-syllable word.

**12** This word contains all five common vowels (A, E, I, O, and U), though not necessarily in order.

**13** Every letter in this word appears exactly twice.

**14** If you remove the first letter of this word, the remaining letters will spell a word with the same meaning as the original word.

| | | | |
|---|---|---|---|
| AMBIDEXTROUS | CROSSWORD | INTESTINES | RUST |
| AREA | CRUDE | LEAST | SHOUT |
| BOOKKEEPER | DETECTED | MARS | STRAW |
| CHEAT | HERE | PRAISING | THORN |

When you're done, surprise! The last word remaining will be *almost* last . . .

# LAW AND REORDER

This puzzle has two parts. First, name the six pictures and figure out where to put the words in the crossword. Then, transfer the letters from the crossword to the numbered boxes at the bottom to get the answer to the riddle.

**Q** Why did the police arrest the great actor after the performance?

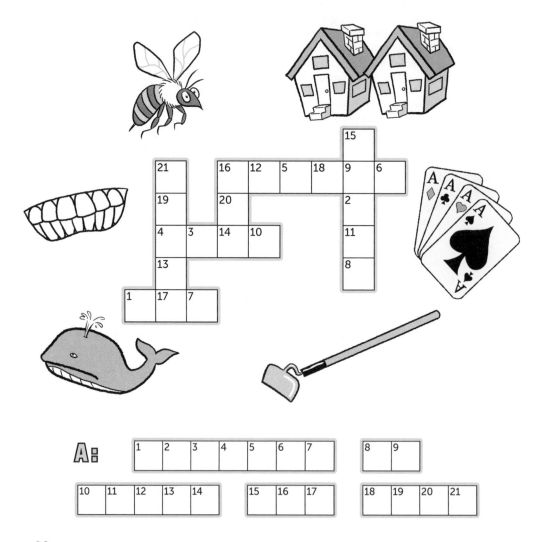

# LIST BREAKERS

Each of these lists has been translated into its own code. In the first list, for example, a D represents N, so fill in N wherever you see a D. Hint: Start by thinking of something that might fit into one of the lists, then see if any of the entries have that same letter pattern. If a letter appears in two places in the word, its coded substitute will do the same. (For hints on solving this kind of code, see Code Hard Facts.)

## THINGS AT A PICNIC

**EXAMPLE:** PLASTIC FORKS
**HINT:** Every D is an N.

1  Y I B O W R O T S D

2  J S W D   S D   B U O   J S P

3  B I P T O J T S B U

4  N W C L B   F I T I K

5  A I A O W   A T I B O F

6  N W L O K   J U L J X O D

7  X O B J U C A

8  U I R P C W V O W   P C D F

9  A S B I B S   J U L A F

10  D I A X L D F

## HALLOWEEN COSTUMES

**EXAMPLE:** VAMPIRE
**HINT:** Every G is an N.

1  T Q S E F

2  K X J G N Z G I S Z Q G

3  C M D P Z X B J E N

4  G Q G B J

5  I N Z C Z S L G

6  T Q U J X V

7  I M R Z X F Z X L

8  R L C Q E Z   L K K Q E Z X

9  F Z J V C Z I I   F L X I Z D J G

10  U L D P Q Z

# LISTEN HERE

Each list of words below will sound like someplace you've heard of if you say them out loud. For example, in the category of US states, a list of the words "Sow, with, duck, code, huh" sounds like "South Dakota." How many can you get? Hint: If you get stuck, try having somebody say the words to you.

## US STATES

1  Pencil, vein, yeah _____

2  Eel, annoy _____

3  Arrows, owner _____

4  Kinetic, hut _____

5  Row, dial, and _____

6  Tennis, he _____

7  Whisk, on, sun _____

## COUNTRIES OF THE WORLD

1  Chair, money _____

2  Sink, up, oar _____

3  Sweets, hurl, end _____

4  Fur, ants _____

5  He, chipped _____

6  You, rig, why _____

7  Tile, hand _____

## US TOURIST ATTRACTIONS

1  Nigh, hag, rough, halls
_____

2  Stout, chew, huff, flipper, tea
_____

3  Lean, kin, ma'am, oriole
_____

4  Grant, Kenya, inn
_____

5  Sandy, hay, goes, who
_____

6  Who, furred, ham
_____

7  Goal, ding, hate, burr, itch
_____

## BODIES OF WATER

1  Legs, hoop, airier
_____

2  Pen, him, muck, hen, owl
_____

3  Pass, if, hick, go, shun
_____

4  Made, it, tar, rainy, hens, he
_____

5  Golf, huff, make, sick, hoe
_____

6  Mrs., hippie, riff, her
_____

7  Chess, or, peek, pay
_____

# LOOK BOTH WAYS BEFORE CROSSING

## WORD SQUARES

**L**ook at these four words:

Now take a look at them again—this time reading *down*.

|   |   |   |   |
|---|---|---|---|
| F | I | N | D |
| I | D | E | A |
| N | E | W | T |
| D | A | T | E |

That's a *word square*: a group of words that read the same both across and down.

Word squares have a long history. A 5 × 5 word square, called the Sator Square (below), was even found carved into a wall in the ruins of Pompeii. This square is interesting for a number of reasons. For one, the words make a sentence when they're read in order. (Roughly translated, it means "The farmer Arepo uses his plow to work.") For another, the words can be read across and down, down and up, forward *and* backward. Some historians say that, back in the days of Pompeii, people believed a word square would protect a house by confusing the Devil. (Sorry, Pompeii, but it didn't work.)

|   |   |   |   |   |
|---|---|---|---|---|
| S | A | T | O | R |
| A | R | E | P | O |
| T | E | N | E | T |
| O | P | E | R | A |
| R | O | T | A | S |

Much more recently, a computer program designed to make word squares with seven-letter words was only able to come up with 52 examples. However, the program was not clever enough to take a four-letter word like LOOK and turn it into longer words like LOOKING, LOOKERS, and so on. This would give many more possibilities.

Here is a lovely 7 × 7 square that was made without the help of a computer program—in fact it was made in 1882. (REGATTA, in the third spot, is a common word for a boat race.)

|   |   |   |   |   |   |   |
|---|---|---|---|---|---|---|
| M | E | R | G | E | R | S |
| E | T | E | R | N | A | L |
| R | E | G | A | T | T | A |
| G | R | A | V | I | T | Y |
| E | N | T | I | T | L | E |
| R | A | T | T | L | E | R |
| S | L | A | Y | E | R | S |

If you write a word square of your own, you might want to start small . . . but not too small. A 4 × 4 square is relatively easy to make—there are likely millions of possibilities. Using four-letter words is actually easier than using three-letter words, for one simple reason: English has about four times as many four-letter words to choose from. Just remember to look both ways before crossing.

Here's an incomplete 4 × 4 word square. Can you place the ten given letters into the grid so that the same words will read across and down?

|   |   |   |   |
|---|---|---|---|
| C |   |   | B |
|   | A |   |   |
|   |   | T |   |
| B |   |   | T |

**A A C C E E S S R R**

*For some puzzles with word squares like these, see Aha!, Color Scheme, What's the Buzz?, and Yuck!*

# LOOK OUT BELOW!

The letters spelling DANGER ZONE are hidden in this chaotic scene. The letters will be different sizes and may be turned, but they'll look like the ones shown below. Can you find each letter?

# LUMBER PARTY

The panels in this comic strip are shown out of order. Number the blank circles with the correct order so the strip tells a funny story.

 **THE PUZZLE**

There are eight US states that begin with the letter M. Using these clues, can you identify seven of those state names and fit them into the grid on the next page? When you are done, the eighth state's name will appear in the shaded column.

**1**

Hide-and-seek players sometimes say this state's name after each number when counting.

The state is named after the largest river in the United States.

Most of the catfish in the United States come from this state.

**2**

The heart of Kansas City is located in this state—not in Kansas.

One of its most famous landmarks is the Gateway Arch.

The St. Louis Cardinals play at Busch Stadium in this state.

**3**

The largest city in this small state is Baltimore.

It was one of the 13 original colonies.

Some of the area that is now Washington, DC, was originally part of this state.

**4**

This state's baseball team is called the Twins, and its football team is the Vikings.

Its nickname is Land of 10,000 Lakes, although it actually has closer to 12,000.

Some place names in this state like Minneiska and Minnetonka come from the Dakota language (the Dakota word minne means "water").

**5**

Its capital is Boston.

The first Thanksgiving feast was held at Plymouth in what is now this state.

The eastern end of this state looks like a bent arm, or a hook, that juts into the Atlantic Ocean.

**6**

This is the only state whose name consists of just one syllable.

On a map of the United States, this state is located in the upper right corner.

It's known for its lobster.

**7**

This state is bordered by four of the five Great Lakes, one of which has the same name as the state.

The largest city in this state is Detroit.

The Wolverines, a college football team, play in the largest stadium in the United States, located in this state.

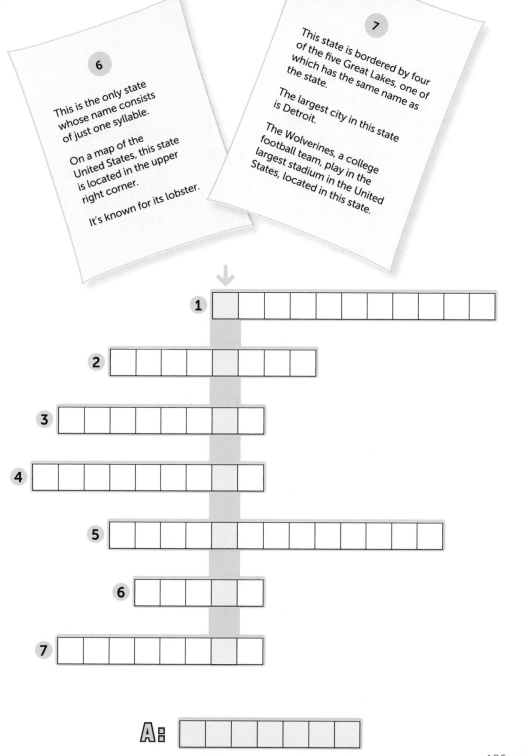

# MADE TO ORDER

Can you figure out which dishes this restaurant is serving? For each of the food categories, examine the nine trios of letters. Then, keeping the letters in the same order within each trio, place the trios into the blanks to get three nine-letter foods. All of the trios for each category are mixed together. One of the trios has been placed to help you get started.

## Breakfast Foods

| EFR | ANT | DOU |
|-----|-----|-----|
| GHN | CRO | IES |
| ISS | UTS | HOM |

_ _ _ G H N _ _ _

_ _ _ _ _ _ _ _ _

_ _ _ _ _ _ _ _ _

## Main Courses

| GER | TTI | BCA |
|-----|-----|-----|
| KES | HAM | GHE |
| CRA | SPA | BUR |

_ _ _ _ _ _ _ _ _

_ _ _ _ _ _ _ _ _

_ _ _ _ _ _ _ _ _

## Ice-Cream Flavors

| KYR | PIS | COL |
|-----|-----|-----|
| HIO | OAD | CHO |
| TAC | ATE | ROC |

_ _ _ _ _ _ _ _ _

_ _ _ _ _ _ _ _ _

_ _ _ _ _ _ _ _ _

# MATCH MAKING

To get the riddle's answer, examine these workers and match them to the things they work on. Use a ruler to draw a line connecting the dots between them. Each line you draw will cross out one of the letters in the circles. When you've got all the matches, the remaining letters will spell the answer to the riddle.

**Q:** **What do candlemakers work on that almost nobody else works on?**

(W) (I) (N) (A) (C) (T) (S) (K) (U) (L) (E) (R) (N) (D) (O) (S)

**A:** _____

# MAZES THAT GROW ON YOU

## THE WINDING WORLD OF HEDGE MAZES

In this word-filled maze, start at the word EVER and continue along the paths till you get to the lawn mower in the center. The correct path will explain all about hedge mazes, but incorrect turns will take you down dead ends and give you nonsense information.

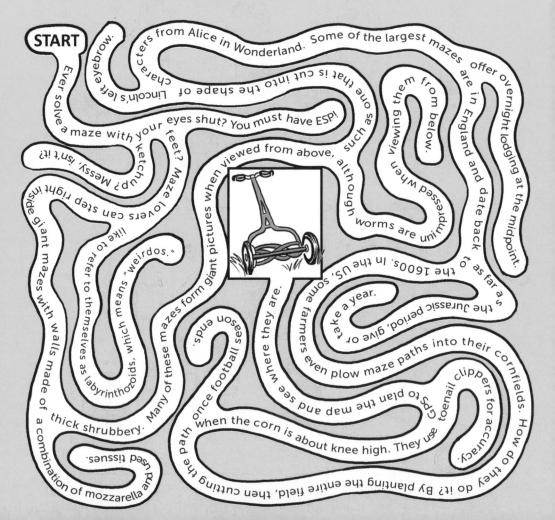

START

# MIND YOUR P'S AND Q'S

The phrase "mind your p's and q's" is an old expression that means "mind your manners," but in this puzzle, it's about the letters. Each sentence below has two blanks. Fill in the first blank with a word that contains the letter P. Fill in the second blank with that same word—except replace the P with the letters Q-U to make a new word. For example, SPIRE in the first blank would become SQUIRE in the second. Can you get them all?

**1** Every time the actress started to _____ , some rude man in the audience made his chair _____ .

**2** When my friend stayed for dinner, he ate only a small _____ of his meal but then finished an entire _____ of our ice cream!

**3** You can _____ whomever you'd like for your team, but please be _____ about it because it'll be getting dark soon.

**4** We had a _____ tire in the trunk, but it was so deformed it looked more _____ than round.

**5** Those cherry _____ will keep making the dog sick until he _____ eating them.

**6** With my new easel and brushes, I may try to _____ a cottage by the lake or something _____ like that.

**7** The farmer was just about to _____ his car with luggage when he heard a _____ come from the back seat.

# MIXED MESSAGES

In each of these anagram puzzles, all the letters in the top row will appear in a different order in the bottom row, spelling a phrase related to the original message. For example, all the letters in ASTRONOMER would be rearranged to spell the related phrase MOON STARER. Only some boxes have a connection line showing what letters go where. Work back and forth between top and bottom to place every letter. It might help to cross out each top letter once you've placed it in the bottom.

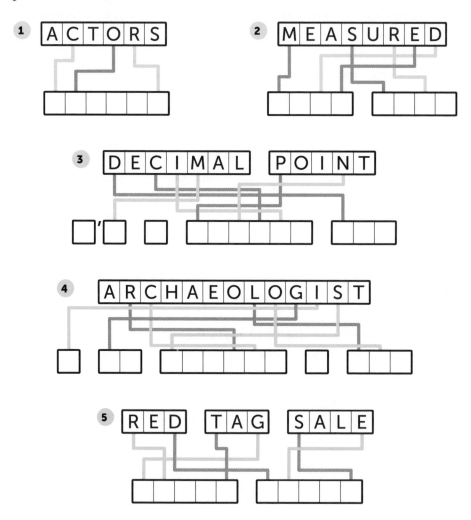

# MONEY TALKS

Each piece of paper here represents an IOU (that is, an "I owe you" note). Examine each scene and think of a phrase that describes it, starting the words with the letters IOU (in order), like Inchworm Organizing Uniforms.

# MOVIE CREW

Quiet on the set! This grid contains words from the world of moviemaking, which are listed below. When you've found them all, read the leftover letters (from left to right, top to bottom) to get an Interesting Fact.

```
D  T  S  H  O  L  L  Y  W  O  O  D  B  E  I
E  C  H  T  T  R  I  A  E  R  P  O  N  N  C
G  O  O  A  U  O  R  N  W  U  O  E  T  I  O
A  S  O  P  T  D  L  R  E  M  C  T  S  D  L
T  T  T  R  R  S  I  K  R  S  F  D  C  N  I
S  U  I  O  A  L  A  O  C  T  C  I  M  A  G
D  M  B  D  I  M  M  W  W  A  O  R  V  T  H
N  E  I  U  L  E  S  C  R  R  B  E  I  S  T
U  S  T  C  E  F  F  E  L  A  I  C  E  P  S
O  E  N  E  R  E  M  I  S  O  P  T  U  T  T
S  P  O  R  P  A  O  F  L  O  S  O  E  U  R
D  T  S  A  C  T  I  O  N  M  E  R  C  R  R
```

| | | | |
|---|---|---|---|
| ACTION | CUT | PROPS | STAR |
| ACTOR | DIRECTOR | SCENE | STUDIO |
| BACK LOT | FILM | SCRIPT | THAT'S A WRAP |
| BOOM | HOLLYWOOD | SETS | TRAILER |
| CAMERA | LIGHTS | SHOOT | WARDROBE |
| CAST | LINES | SOUNDSTAGE | WRITER |
| COSTUMES | MAKEUP | SPECIAL EFFECTS | |
| CREW | PRODUCER | STAND-IN | |

## INTERESTING FACT:

— — — — — — —   — — — —   — — — —

— — — — — —   — — —   — —   — — — — .

112

# THE PUZZLE

Each item on the left can become an item on the right if an N is added. (For example, PRICE could become PRINCE.) Use a ruler to connect the dots of the pictures that go together. Each line will cross out some of the circled letters in the middle. Read the leftover letters from top to bottom to get the riddle's answer.

**Q:** What short word becomes long just by adding an N?

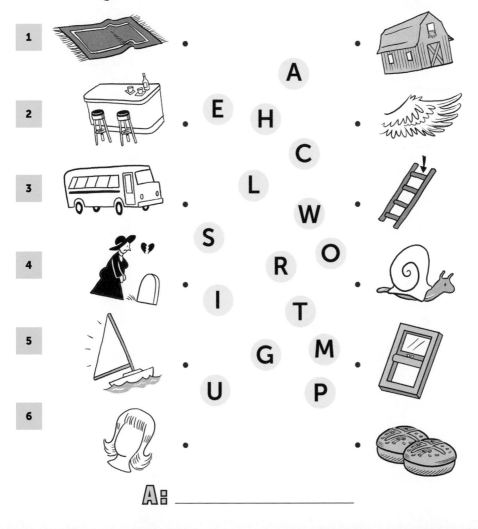

**A:** _____

# NAMING NAMES

You'll need to use your sense of humor for this one. Match each job with a first and last name so that, when the full name is said out loud, it sounds related to the occupation in some way. For example, a mattress salesperson might be named Anita Knapp, which sounds like "I need a nap."

| OCCUPATIONS | FIRST NAME | LAST NAME |
|---|---|---|
| 1 Chemist | _____ | _____ |
| 2 Eye doctor | _____ | _____ |
| 3 First-grade teacher | _____ | _____ |
| 4 Furniture restorer | _____ | _____ |
| 5 Gardener | _____ | _____ |
| 6 Locksmith | _____ | _____ |
| 7 Paleontologist | _____ | _____ |
| 8 Physical-education teacher | _____ | _____ |
| 9 Plumber | _____ | _____ |
| 10 Prison warden | _____ | _____ |
| 11 Singer | _____ | _____ |
| 12 Thief | _____ | _____ |

## FIRST NAMES

| | | | | | |
|---|---|---|---|---|---|
| Barb | Dan | Doug | Kent | Molly | Rhea |
| Carrie | Doris | Jim | Lee | Reed | Robin |

## LAST NAMES

| | | | | | |
|---|---|---|---|---|---|
| Banks | DeLyon | Enright | King | Polster | Shortz |
| Boanes | Dwyer | Kewel | Oakey | Seawell | Tuck |

# NATURE TRAIL

See if you can find your way through this nature maze. Move left, right, up, or
down (but not diagonally) to the next picture only if it is either the same color
(black, gray, or yellow) or the same image as the one you're on. Start on the gray
acorn in the upper left corner. From there, you may move either to the gray leaf
next to it or to the black acorn below it. Keep moving until you reach the gray leaf
in the bottom right corner.

**START**

# NEOLOGISMS

## WHAT'S THE LATEST WORD?

Every word we write or speak comes from somewhere, of course, but some words evolve over time (see Word Origins: Strange Etymologies), while others seem to pop up out of the blue.

William Shakespeare often found that the English language did not have words that were colorful or expressive enough to say what he meant. So he invented what he needed, usually by altering or combining existing words. Some of the many hundreds of words and phrases we still use today that were created or popularized by Shakespeare are:

| | |
|---|---|
| cold-blooded | leapfrog |
| dead as a doornail | mind's eye |
| good riddance | one fell swoop |
| lackluster | wild-goose chase |

A newly invented word is called a *coinage* or *neologism* (from the Greek *neo* meaning "new" and *logos* meaning "word"). Words are often coined when something is invented or discovered. For example, *robot* is a coinage: It was introduced by a Czech science-fiction author from a Czech word for someone forced to work. *Hashtag* comes from *hash mark*, another name for the pound sign, and *tag*, meaning "identifier."

Some coinages started as brand names, abbreviations, or combinations of words (see Brunch Is Served: Portmanteau Words). In 1900, the word *escalator* was invented to be the brand name for a moving staircase (and it was intended to be pronounced "es-CAL-ator"). In the 1920s, when cars made long-distance travel popular, *motel* was coined by blending the words *motor* and *hotel*. And in the 1950s, when swimmers began to carry a tank of oxygen underwater, they needed a name shorter than "self-contained underwater breathing apparatus." So they took the first letter of each word in that phrase to form an acronym: *scuba*.

Here's how a portmanteau word started as a brand name and wound up as a coinage. In 1937, the Hormel company needed a brand name for its spiced ham product. It combined the first two letters of *spiced* with the last two of *ham* to form *Spam*. In 1970, the comedy show *Monty Python's Flying Circus* featured a sketch about a restaurant in which every item on the menu was made with Spam. The waitress in the sketch listed a dish's ingredients as "Spam, Spam, Spam, Spam, Spam, Spam, baked beans, Spam, Spam, Spam . . . " (The word *Spam* is mentioned at least 132 times during the sketch.) Years later, the endless and unwanted stream of messages that kept showing up in email inboxes came to be compared to the Spam in that sketch, and it became a new word.

What word for the number 1 followed by a hundred zeros was coined by a nine-year-old boy? (Hint: That word, with a new spelling, is now a word that means "to search on the internet.")

# NO COACHING!

This puzzle has two parts. First, name the eight pictures and figure out where to put the words in the crossword. Then transfer the letters from the crossword to the numbered boxes at the bottom to get the answer to the riddle. Hint: Start by finding the best spots for both five-letter words.

**Q:** Why did the royal coachman worry that he'd get a flat tire?

# NOT EGGS-ACTLY

Only two of these scenes are eggs-actly alike. Can you find the pair, and spot the differences in the others?

# NOTE WORTHY

These kids are choosing which instruments to learn to play. Use the clues and logic to match each kid to their new instrument. Some kids may like more than one instrument, but there is only one way that all of the kids will have an instrument.

**BITA** has asthma and will only play an instrument you don't blow.

She'll play _____ .

**JUSTIN** wants to play a percussion instrument.

He'll play _____ .

**KATIE** doesn't want to worry about replacing strings on her instrument.

She'll play _____ .

**MICHAEL** will play anything, but not the same instrument as his twin brother, Tim.

He'll play _____ .

**TIM** wants to play something that starts with the same letter as his first name.

He'll play _____ .

**VALERIE** wants an instrument small enough to carry in her backpack.

She'll play _____ .

# NOTHING BUT NET

The things listed below will fit into these boxes so that the words all interlock like a crossword puzzle. But everywhere the letters N-E-T appear together in the words, they have been replaced in the grid with a picture of a net. Can you put the words in their correct spots by using their lengths and the places where they cross as a guide? (Ignore punctuation and spaces between words.)

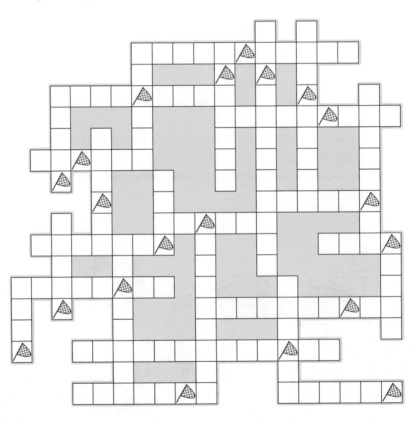

| | | | |
|---|---|---|---|
| BONNET | FORTUNE-TELLER | MARIE ANTOINETTE | PLANET |
| BRUNETTE | HAIRNET | MARIONETTE | PLANE TICKET |
| CABINET | IMAGINE THAT! | NETHERLANDS | SAFETY NET |
| CANINE TEETH | INTERNET | NETTLED | TV NETWORKS |
| CASTANETS | JASMINE TEA | NINETEEN | UNETHICAL |
| CLARINET | LUNCHEONETTE | PHONETIC | VENETIAN BLINDS |
| FINE-TUNE | MAGNET | PINE TREE | |

# NOW HEAR THIS!

Loud enough for you? It should be! Hidden in this grid are the noisy words listed below. When you've found them all, read the leftover letters (from left to right, top to bottom) to get an Interesting Fact.

```
C  L  A  C  K  C  A  W  H  T  P  S
I  R  N  N  Z  P  O  D  N  G  P
I  H  U  K  A  B  O  O  M  U  S  L
N  L  S  N  Z  A  G  O  M  E  H  A
C  D  F  I  C  O  N  R  M  T  W  T
R  H  N  L  W  H  O  O  S  H  H  E
A  G  M  P  S  S  D  G  O  U  A  U
C  N  D  A  P  S  G  O  N  F  M  P
K  E  R  P  L  U  N  K  T  I  O  E
L  N  O  H  O  B  I  N  G  O  O  E
E  W  O  E  P  G  D  A  F  M  R  B
S  S  I  H  C  E  E  R  C  S  V  E
```

| | | | |
|---|---|---|---|
| BEEP | CRUNCH | PLOP | THUNK |
| BING | DING-DONG | POOF | THWACK |
| BLAM | HISS | POW | VROOM |
| BOING | HONK | SCREECH | WHAM |
| CLACK | KABOOM | SPLAT | WHOOSH |
| CLUNK | KERPLUNK | SWISH | ZING |
| CRACKLE | PLINK | THUD | ZOOM |

## INTERESTING FACT:

\_\_ \_\_ \_\_ \_\_ - \_\_ \_\_ \_\_ \_\_   \_\_ \_\_   \_\_ \_\_ \_\_ \_\_ \_\_

\_\_ \_\_ \_\_   \_\_ \_\_ \_\_ \_\_ \_\_

\_\_ \_\_   \_\_ \_\_ \_\_   \_\_ \_\_ \_\_ \_\_ .

# NUMBER CRUNCHING

## THE BEALE CIPHERS

It's 1885, and a stranger tells you a dramatic story about a series of unsolved codes that could reveal the hiding spot of nearly $45 million in buried treasure. For 50 cents, the stranger sells you a pamphlet called *The Beale Papers* that shares the codes and tells the story of the treasure.

The story goes like this: Way back in the 1820s, a man named Thomas Beale rode into a Virginia town to bury a priceless treasure. Before he left town, Beale made friends with hotel operator Robert Morriss, and gave him a locked iron box. Beale told Morriss that if he didn't return in ten years, Morriss should open the box and solve the three codes inside, which would lead him to the treasure. Beale said the codes would be "unintelligible without the aid of a key," which he had left with someone else. He didn't say what the key was—or who had it.

According to the pamphlet, Morriss waited 23 years before opening the box. Inside he found three densely numbered codes. For 20 years he tried to decipher them without the key. Shortly before he died, he showed the papers to a friend, who had an amazing idea. He numbered all 1,322 words in the Declaration of Independence to see if they corresponded with the numbers in any of the codes. In the second code, the first number is 115. The 115th word in the Declaration is INSTITUTED, which begins with I. Could the first letter of the code, then, be I?

He was right. The Declaration of Independence was the key. He solved the entire middle cipher, which described a buried vault and its nearly priceless contents—but not its location.

He never did solve the other two ciphers. To this day, they remain unsolved, despite the efforts of top cryptographers and powerful computers. One man started working on them in 1923 and continued into the 1970s!

Could the whole story about Beale and his hidden treasure be made up just to get you to buy the pamphlet? It's possible. If the story and the other two ciphers are fake, that would explain why they've never been solved. Plus, there's not much evidence that Beale actually existed. Skeptics point out that a letter, supposedly from 1822 and reprinted in the pamphlet, contains *stampede*, a word that didn't appear in print until 1834.

But whether or not the Beale ciphers are a hoax, consider this true story: A stranger just sold you a 23-page pamphlet for the 1885 equivalent of about $15. And you're not the only curious person who's bought one. The stranger probably hasn't made $45 million yet, but it's a start.

Are you thinking of devoting your life to finding Beale's hidden treasure? Using the text in this Puzzle Breaker, apply the deciphering method explained above to decode this advice before you get started:

9, 14, 24, 6, 16, 14, 15, 24, 6, 14, 24, 1, 6

# THE PUZZLE

The things listed below will fit into these boxes so that the words all interlock like a crossword puzzle. All the words have O as their only vowel. By using the lengths of the words and the places where they cross as a guide, can you put them all in the correct spots? (Ignore punctuation and spaces between words.) Some words may fit in different places, but there is only one way to complete the entire grid.

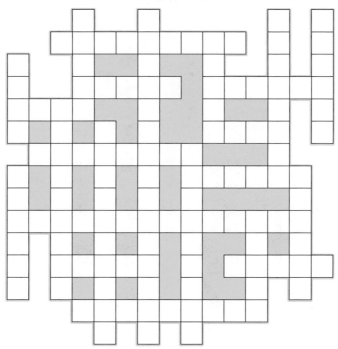

| BONGOS | HO, HO, HO! | POLO |
| BOWWOW | HONOR ROLL | POT OF GOLD |
| COLOR | HOP ON POP | ROBOT |
| COTTON BOWL | HOW NOW, BROWN COW | SLO-MO |
| CROOK | LOCO | TOP DOG |
| CROSSWORD | LOTTO | TORSO |
| FROM TOP TO BOTTOM | ODD JOB | TWO O'CLOCK |
| GOOD TO GO | OSLO | |

# OBSTACLE COURSE

First, use a ruler to connect the dots in numerical order. Then draw a path from the runner to the trophy at the end. The correct path will cross at least one of each type of obstacle. For an extra challenge, close your eyes when you reach each one and (with your pencil) try to jump over the sandbox, zigzag through the cones, touch every rung on the monkey bars, swim straight through the water course, and jump over each hurdle.

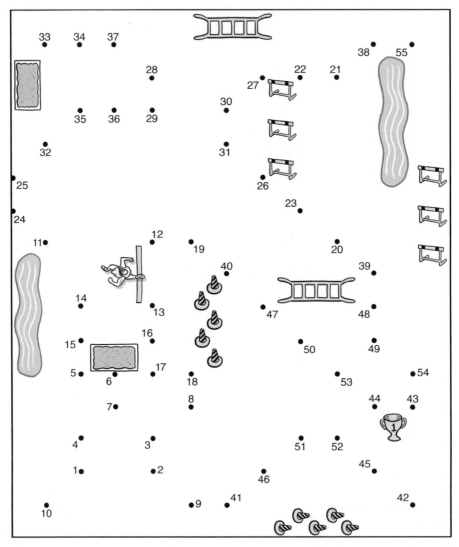

# O, I C!

This word search may seem tricky, but it's E-Z-R than it looks. Simply sound out each entry in the list below to discover the words and phrases hidden in the grid. For example, CL is found in the grid as SEAL, and T42 is hidden as TEA FOR TWO. To help you solve, the list is given so the spelled-out answers are in alphabetical order. When you've found them all, read the leftover letters (from left to right, top to bottom) to get a Bonus Message.

```
E  Y  E  O  T  E  Y  E  E  E  S  E  A  S  Y
L  U  R  O  M  K  E  C  A  H  N  E  N  M  H
E  E  A  P  N  E  N  I  T  H  E  E  A  E  W
V  X  T  E  A  F  O  R  T  W  O  L  R  L  H
A  Y  C  N  D  R  Y  Y  O  U  N  A  L  G  O
T  R  E  E  S  D  N  A  T  I  A  W  U  O  Y
O  E  A  M  S  L  A  N  I  G  I  R  O  V  H
R  L  O  Y  K  S  A  Y  O  R  P  Y  N  O  W
U  R  O  E  N  O  M  E  N  A  A  E  S  C  K
```

| | | | |
|---|---|---|---|
| NE1 | _____ | LO | _____ |
| DL | _____ | RHNL | _____ |
| EZ | _____ | PNO | _____ |
| LF8R | _____ | CNMNE | _____ |
| MT | _____ | CL | _____ |
| NME | _____ | CI2I | _____ |
| NRG | _____ | T42 | _____ |
| NV | _____ | YOY | _____ |
| XS | _____ | U8NC | _____ |

## BONUS MESSAGE:

___ ___ ___ ___    ___ ___ ___    ___ ___ ___ ___

___ ___ ___ ___ " ___ ___ ___ ___ ___    ___ ___ ___ ___ "

___ ___ " ___ ___ ___ ___ ___    ___ ___ ___ ___ " ___ ___ ___ .

# ONE, TWO, THREE

In this unusual crossword, each box may hold one, two, or three letters. For example, the first Across answer word, COUPON, is spread over three consecutive boxes containing COU, PO, and N, while the first Down answer word crossing it will use that COU chunk. The number of letters to use in each box is shown with gray ovals—use one oval per letter.

## ACROSS

| 1 | It's scanned at checkout to lower an item's price |
| 4 | Bursts of lightning |
| 7 | Kitchen appliance |
| 8 | If you fling this, it might return to you |
| 9 | Fitting together, like jigsaw pieces |
| 11 | Word on a red sign |
| 12 | Largest bird in the world |
| 15 | _____ a bit (to a large degree) |

| 17 | This person shows you to your seat at a play |
| 19 | "Magic word" at the dinner table |
| 20 | Woolly South American animal |
| 22 | Caribbean island whose capital is Havana |
| 24 | Reptile that "announces" when it is about to strike |
| 28 | Barbed item some people put a worm on |
| 30 | Private, daily journal |
| 31 | Amount equal to four quarts |
| 32 | Lots and lots |

| # | Clue |
|---|------|
| 1 | The child of your aunt and uncle |
| 2 | Last name of Harry who went to Hogwarts |
| 3 | Long works of fiction |
| 4 | Long-necked pink birds |
| 5 | Transparent, like fabric |
| 6 | Performed a musical number with your voice |
| 8 | Item on a library shelf |
| 10 | Eight-armed sea creature |
| 13 | Hit in which the runner gets to third base |
| 14 | Run after |
| 15 | Porcupine needle |
| 16 | Hot drink you might put lemon into |
| 18 | Super-strong character from Greek mythology |
| 21 | Footrace that's usually over 26 miles long |
| 23 | Outlaw from the Old West |
| 25 | Grabbed and kept |
| 26 | Vice President Burr who killed Alexander Hamilton in a duel |
| 27 | Lock openers |
| 28 | _____ Newtons (cookie brand) |
| 29 | Formal way of saying "will" |

Crossword grid:

1 C O 2 P O 3 N

# ON THE HOUSE

Fill in each row of boxes with the name of one of the objects shown. Some letters have been placed to get you started. When you've filled every box, read down the two columns of shaded boxes to discover the answer to the riddle.

**Q:** What's the best way for a carpenter to do his job exactly right?

**A:** _ _ _   _ _ _ _   _ _ _ _

_ _   _ _ _   _ _ _ _ .

# OPPOSITE DAY

This puzzle started with eleven pairs of opposites. A letter from the first word in each pair has been switched with a letter from the second word to make two new words. For example, YEN and SO become the opposites YES and NO once the N and S are switched back. The switched letters can come from anywhere in either word. Can you find all the pairs of opposites?

YEN / SO → **YES** / **NO**

FIT / THAN → _____ / _____

COAL / WORM → _____ / _____

FLESH / STARE → _____ / _____

SAPPY / HAD → _____ / _____

LOFT / SOUND → _____ / _____

WED / TRY → _____ / _____

SHARD / PULL → _____ / _____

DIVE / LIE → _____ / _____

FAN / REAR → _____ / _____

FEED / HEAT → _____ / _____

# OUT ON A LIMB

Each of these sentences has the name of a bird hidden somewhere inside. All the names are hidden across two or more words. For example, in the first sentence, SWAN appears in WAS WANDERING. Can you find the bird in each sentence?

**1** The little bird was wandering along the beach, looking for grubs.

**2** Most rich countries can afford to set aside land where birds can safely rest along their migratory routes.

**3** The bird's sudden dive reminded us of a plane flaming out after engine failure.

**4** Unlike the illustration on a dollar bill, it's unlikely that a real bird can clasp arrows in its claws.

**5** The chapel I canoed past during my birdwatching expedition had several nests in the bell tower.

**6** The young chick made its first attempt to leave its nest with awkward flaps of its little wings.

**7** You can find the state bird on a postcard in almost every state's welcome center.

**8** Many birds had already flown south for the winter, so the snowstorm wasn't as big a catastrophe as anticipated.

**9** A baby bird that has fallen to the ground should be returned to its nest or kept safe until its mother returns.

# OXYMORONS

## JUMBO SHRIMP AND OTHER INSTANT CLASSICS

Oxymorons, in addition to having a very funny name, are also funny to think about. An *oxymoron* is a phrase made of a contradiction that is usually overlooked. "Pretty ugly," for example, is made up of two words that are almost exactly opposites. ("Almost exactly" is another oxymoron—something can't be "almost" anything if it is "exactly" that thing.)

Have you ever been given the "smaller half" of something? Halves are supposed to be equal—so how is that possible? And how could someone be an "uninvited guest," since a guest is a person who is invited? Or, for that matter, how can a TV show have a "guest host"? All of these are oxymorons. (The word oxymoron, by the way, comes from two Greek words meaning "sharp" and "dull." Guess which part means "dull"!)

Just as Shakespeare added new words to English (see Neologisms: What's the Latest Word?), he also introduced many oxymoronic phrases. Perhaps the best-known comes from *Romeo and Juliet*: "Parting is such *sweet sorrow*."

**On the right are two lists of words in random order. (Come to think of it, how can a random list be in order?) Pair the words on the left with the words on the right to get nine "strangely familiar" oxymoronic phrases.**

PAID

UNBELIEVABLY

GROWING

FINAL

STRANGELY

SECOND

COMPLETELY

DEAFENING

AWFULLY

FAMILIAR

SILENCE

DRAFT

BEST

REALISTIC

GOOD

VOLUNTEER

SMALLER

UNFINISHED

# THE PUZZLE

Eight animals whose names begin with P are shown here. First, identify the animals and write each name in the only row where it will fit. When you're done, the name of another animal, whose first letter is *not* P, will appear from top to bottom in one of the columns. Write the name on the line below, then change that animal's first letter—and the *other* instance of that letter—to P. You'll reveal yet another animal's name.

A: _____ → _____

132

# PAIR-OFFS

To find the answer to this riddle, start by identifying the seven pictures and writing their names in the boxes. Next, look at all the letters and cross off all the pairs—that is, any letters that appear more than once, even if they appear in different words. The remaining letters, in order, will spell the riddle's answer.

**Q:** If you lose your swim trunks at the beach, what should you go home in?

**A:** _____

# PANGRAMS

## FROM A TO Z

## The quick brown fox jumps over a lazy dog.

That may not be a remarkable occurrence (unless you're the fox or the dog), but it is a remarkable sentence, and here's why: Although it contains only 33 letters, every letter of the alphabet appears at least once. That makes it a *pangram*. (*Pan* means "all" and *gram* means "something written.")

Not every letter of the alphabet is equally common. If you took a random page from a book and examined the first 1,000 letters, about 127 of them would be E and about 90 would be T, the two most common letters. But only one of them is likely to be a Z. Even the letter X is more common than Z, although it almost never shows up at the start of a word (which is why the X section of a dictionary is so short).

Typesetters, who used to assemble the metal letters used to print books and newspapers by hand, noticed these different letter frequencies as they worked. Single letters were carved onto individual pieces of metal, and typesetters would set one piece next to another to form words and paragraphs. It didn't take them long to notice that they ran out of Es before anything else.

(By the way, typesetters kept their letters in two cases: one for all the capitals and another for the smaller letters. Because they kept the capitals above the smaller ones, these letters came to be called "uppercase" and "lowercase," which is how we still refer to them today.)

Since some letters make it into the mix very infrequently, writing a short pangram is justifiably prized. (In fact, that last sentence is a pangram, but with 87 letters it has lots of repeats.) Not only is it hard to get uncommon letters like J, Q, X, and Z in there, it's also hard to write a pangram that makes sense and sounds normal.

This one may be the best ever written: NEW JOB: FIX MR. GLUCK'S HAZY TV, PDQ! (PDQ is an abbreviation that means "pretty darn quickly.")

Amazingly, this sentence is only 26 letters long, which means that it contains every letter of the alphabet *only once*. And its meaning is fairly easy to understand ("Hurry up and fix Mr. Gluck's blurry television").

A slightly longer one is PACK MY BOX WITH FIVE DOZEN LIQUOR JUGS, which is 32 letters long, one fewer than the "quick brown fox" sentence on the opposite page.

Pangram lovers keep a sharp gaze for the less common letters, hoping to find groups of words that include all twenty-six just by a quirk of chance. (That was another pangram, but it's 118 letters long.) To give you some idea of how rare this is, a pangram fan named Eric Harshbarger read through the names in every "top ten movies of the week" list compiled since 1982. He was looking for a list of ten movie titles that included every letter of the alphabet at least once. The first list he found was published 32 years later. Harshbarger announced this rare event in an article he titled "Well, Moviegoers, Quite a Krazy Box Office Just Happened."

Guess why he used a K!

**Q** **There is one fifteen-letter English word, which is uncopyrightable, that has no repeated letters. Write that word here:**

**A** _ _ _ _ _ _ _ _ _ _ _ _ _ _ _

For puzzles that use every letter of the alphabet, see Alpha-Cross and Pet Peeve.

# PARTY-HOPPING

To find the answer to this riddle, start by identifying each picture below and writing its name in the correct boxes. Some letters have been placed to get you started. Between each pair is a group of shaded boxes that will spell out a word. When you're done, read these shaded words from top to bottom to get the riddle's answer.

**Q: Why do frog parties sometimes last all night?**

**A:** _____

# PET PEEVE

Carefully follow the numbered instructions to cross out letters in the alphabet below. When you're done, three letters will remain. Rearrange the leftover letters to answer the riddle.

**Q:** What should you name a dog that destroys everything in the house?

1. Cross out the letters that appear on the front of playing cards.

2. Cross out each letter whose name contains more than one syllable.

3. Cross out each vowel that, when written as a capital letter, looks the same both upside down and in a mirror.

4. Cross out each letter that forms a word when it's put in front of "ire" and means something that a boss might do to an employee.

5. Cross out the most common vowel when the names of the planets in our solar system are spelled out.

6. Cross out each consonant that rhymes with the letter E.

7. Cross out the two letters that might be given as choices after the question "Do you like this puzzle?"

8. Cross out each letter that appears twice in a row in any word in Clue 5.

A B C D E F G H I J K L M
N O P Q R S T U V W X Y Z

**A:** _ _ _

137

# PICTURED POSTCARDS

Your friend took an around-the-world tour but only sent back these quickly drawn sketches. They don't have much detail, but each should suggest a famous landmark from the trip. Can you identify the landmarks and the countries they're from? Some of them may need to be rotated.

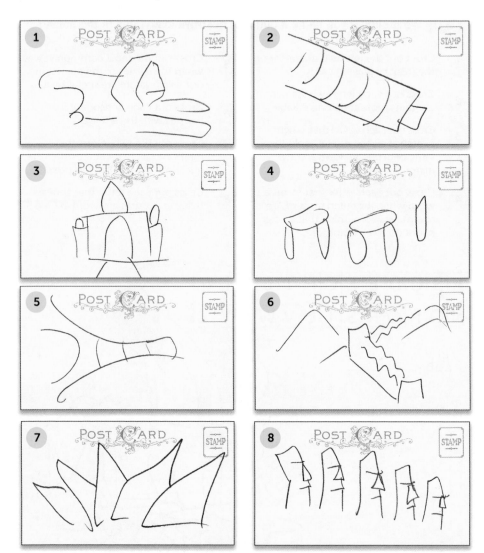

# PINWHEEL

The answer to each clue is a four-letter word. Write each word in the grid in the direction shown by its arrow, starting at the outside and moving in toward the center in an arc. One answer has been filled in to get you started.

1. Three Blind _____ (nursery rhyme)
2. Like a boy, man, bull, or rooster
3. Person who throws a party and greets the guests
4. What Jack and Jill went up and tumbled down
5. Sound from a lion
6. Sway back and forth, like a cradle
7. Performance by actors on a stage
8. What you do when you smile for a camera, or stand still for a painter
9. Common answer to the question "How are you?"
10. A spare tire is a replacement for this
11. Opposite of "die"
12. Person who can't be believed
13. Like a sequoia tree or a skyscraper
14. Extremely small
15. Pedestrians do it
16. A surfboard is designed to ride this

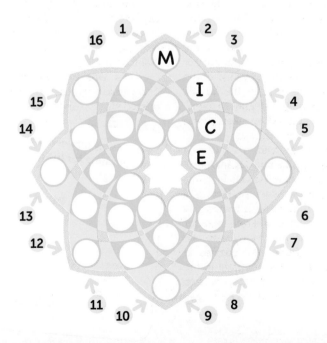

# PLAYING THE NUMBERS

## SUDOKU

One of the biggest puzzle crazes of recent years has been *sudoku*, where solvers fill the numbers 1 through 9 into the rows, columns, and sections of a grid. Today, sudoku puzzles can be found everywhere from daily newspapers to books to phone apps. But before the year 2000, few people in the United States had ever seen a sudoku puzzle.

Although similar puzzles have been around since the late 1800s, the well-known version of sudoku was invented in 1979 by a 74-year-old retired architect from Indiana named Howard Garns. He published these puzzles in an American puzzle magazine under the name Number Place. They weren't an instant hit in the United States, but they became extremely popular in Japan, where they were renamed *su doku*, Japanese for "single number." (Interestingly, even after the Japanese renamed the puzzles, they're still better known in Japan by their English name, Number Place, while English speakers prefer to use the Japanese name, sudoku.)

In 1997, a New Zealand man named Wayne Gould, who was visiting Japan, found a sudoku puzzle in a book. He was instantly hooked, and spent six years perfecting a computer program that could automatically create new sudoku puzzles and rate them for difficulty. Once Gould was happy with the program, he began offering the puzzles to newspapers in Great Britain, and later in the United States, for free. (He wanted people to visit his website to get the solution each day.)

The first of Gould's sudoku puzzles appeared in *The Times* of London on November 12, 2004. The very next day the newspaper's letters section contained a complaint about the puzzle.

What was the complaint? A man had become so engrossed in solving it that he had missed his stop on the train.

---

**How many different orders are possible for the numbers 1 through 9?**

a. 9    b. 81    c. 362,880

---

*For sudoku puzzles with a twist, see Dicedoku and Zoodoku. For other puzzles that use logic to fill in boxes, see Astro-Logical, Hit or Miss, and Rain Check.*

# PLAY IT BY EAR

This waiting room for auditioning singers has something very musical going on. The scene contains four things that start with each of the notes on the musical scale: DO, RE, MI, FA, SO, LA, and TI. For example, the smiling kids depicted on the banner are FACES. Can you get them all?

# POINT BLANK

The answer to each clue is a word or phrase that contains the word UP, DOWN, or both. An arrow appears in place of the direction, with blanks given for the rest of the answer. For example, the clue "Numbers spoken before a launch" would lead to the answer "Countdown," with "down" represented as ↓. See how many you can write ↓ before you give ↑.

**1** Each time you turn the pages of this, a 3-D structure unfolds

___ ___ ___ - ↑   ___ ___ ___ ___

**2** Winter clothing that's filled with feathers to help keep you warm

↓   ___ ___ ___ ___ ___ ___

**3** First this dessert is baked, then it's turned over, and then it's served

↑ ___ ___ ___ ___ - ↓   ___ ___ ___ ___

**4** Phrase made famous by Bugs Bunny

" ___ ___ ___ ___ ' ___   ↑ ,   ___ ___ ___ ?"

**5** Clothing item originally worn by a big brother or sister

___ ___ ___ ___ - ___ ___ - ↓

**6** Not yet decided, like a tossed coin

↑   ___ ___   ___ ___ ___   ___ ___ ___ ___

**7** "Nuclear-strength" temper tantrum

___ ___ ___ ___↓

**8** The umpire shouts this at the start of an inning

" ___ ___ ___ ___ ___ ___   ↑ !"

**9** Put on fancy clothes

___ ___ ___ ___ ___   ↑

**10** Nickname for Australia

↓ ___ ___ ___ ___ ___

**11** Phrase a magician uses before making something appear out of nowhere

" ___ ___ ___ ___ ___ ___ ___ ___ ↑ ___ ___    ___ ___ ___ ___ ___ ___ "

**12** Laughing very hard

___ ___ ___ ___ ___ ___ ___ ___ ↑

**13** This scores six points in football

___ ___ ___ ___ ___ ↓

**14** Proverb that means "Things that go well now won't last forever."

___ ___ ___ ___    ___ ___ ___ ___ ↑ ___ ___ ___ ___

___ ___ ___ ___ ↓

# PRESTO CHOOSE-O

This paragraph is just six sentences long. Choose any word from the first three sentences. Then, starting on the next word, spell out your word, moving one word for each letter. For example, if you start on the word LONG, count CHOOSE, ANY, WORD, and FROM, landing four words later on FROM. Now spell the four letters of FROM, starting on the next word, THE, and keep going in this manner until you can't move any further. We will astoundingly predict your magic last word.

# THE PUZZLE

Are you quite ready to conquer this puzzle? Your quest is to fill the squares in this grid only with words that include a Q. A quick squint will show you that the Qs are already given. Use the cues to fill in the rest.

## ACROSS

**3** Middle Eastern country whose capital is Baghdad

**4** Gemstone with a bluish-green tint

**8** Lower yourself by bending your knees and resting on your heels

**12** Canadian province where many people speak French

**13** Any item that's worth keeping because of its age

**14** Gray, furry-tailed animals that live in trees and eat nuts

**15** Sport played by Hogwarts students

**16** Woman who wears a crown

## DOWN

**1** An abbreviation for lists of questions and answers many people want to know

**2** Give up in the middle

**5** Football team's thrower

**6** Pesky insect that "bites" (but really sucks your blood!)

**7** Explorers need to avoid stepping into this stuff that might make them sink

**9** A new installment of a successful book or movie

**10** Feeling nauseated

**11** Particular, skilled method of performing, painting, etc.

**13** Glass tank for displaying fish

# QUACKING WISE

In this puzzle, you'll be adding and subtracting letters, not numbers. First, identify the pictures. A plus sign means you should write the added picture's name just after the previous one. A minus sign means that instead of adding a word, you should cross out its letters from your string. (Those letters won't usually be in order.) Do each step in the order shown, and the letters remaining, in order, will spell a word. Each answer word can then fit in only one place in the squares by the duck on the next page. The circled letters will reveal the riddle's answer.

**Q** **What did the duck say to the lipstick saleslady?**

1

2

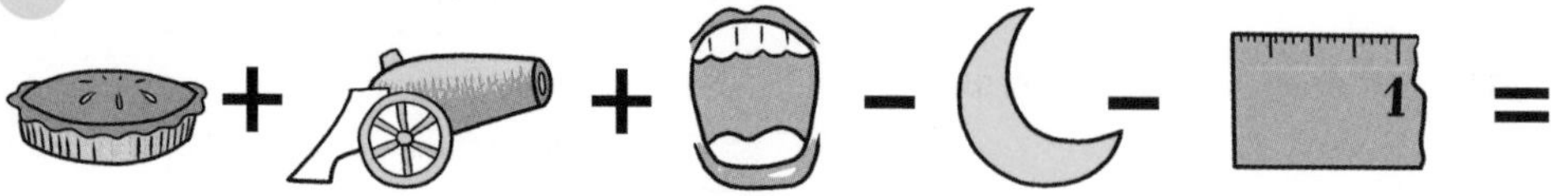

3

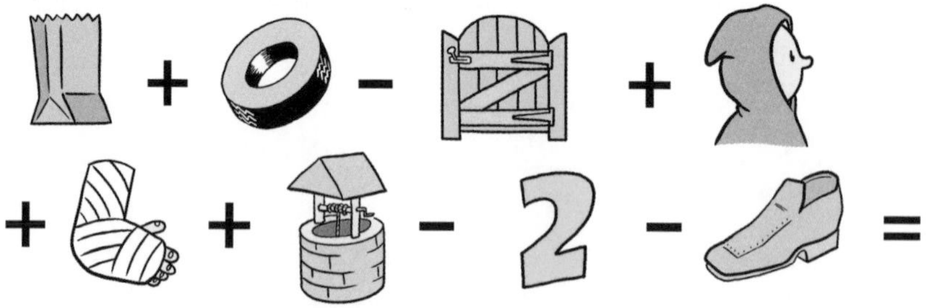

**4**

**5**

A: "_ _ _  _ _  _ _  _ _  _ _ _ _ ."

# QUAD-WRANGLES

In each set of four boxes, choose one letter from each box, in order from left to right, to spell a four-letter word. Do that three more times to get four words that are all members of the same category. (You can only use each letter once.) One word is shown in the first one to get you started.

**1** CATEGORY: _____

| L F | E N | O C | E S |
| K N | O I | P E | K T |

FOOT

**2** CATEGORY: _____

| T O | R A | R U | E A |
| D H | B U | B O | P M |

**3** CATEGORY: _____

| M F | L N | S T | T P |
| W G | O A | A E | A H |

**4** CATEGORY: _____

| S H | I A | A O | N D |
| W R | E N | I N | W T |

**5** CATEGORY: _____

| B M | O I | N Z | W R |
| O R | E U | A O | Z K |

# QUIET!

First, identify each picture and write its name in the blanks. Then determine which letter in each word is silent. Finally, take the silent letters and put them into the matching numbered blanks at the bottom, using the numbers of the pictures, to complete a Japanese proverb. You'll use each silent letter twice.

1 _ _ _ _ _

2 _ _ _ _ _

3 _ _ _ _ _ _

4 _ _ _ _ _ _ _

5 _ _ _ _ _ _

6 _ _ _ _ _

**The** _ _ _ _ _ _ **man is the best to** _ _ _ _ _ _ **to.**
     3  6  4  1  5  2            4  6  3  2  1  5

# QUO-TRIVIA

First, answer as many of the trivia questions as you can. Then transfer the letters to the numbered boxes to reveal a quote by Mark Twain. Work back and forth between the quote and the questions until you have revealed the entire quote.

**1** Who lives in a Gloomy Place at the southeast corner of the Hundred Acre Wood?

| | | | | | |
|---|---|---|---|---|---|

32  51  21  9  4  41

**2** After the moon, the next brightest object we can see in the night sky is which planet?

| | | | | |
|---|---|---|---|---|

31  65  13  59  26

**3** What color is the edible part of a cantaloupe?

| | | | | | |
|---|---|---|---|---|---|

28  67  25  18  73  57

**4** What is a name for a time of day when both hands of a clock point directly upward?

| | | | |
|---|---|---|---|

47  20  38  19

**5** What sport has two varieties that are known as downhill and cross-country?

| | | | | | |
|---|---|---|---|---|---|

60  45  6  22  52  24

**6** What comic strip features Charlie Brown and his dog, Snoopy?

| | | | | | | |
|---|---|---|---|---|---|---|

36  3  43  63  68  27  7

**7** What type of book tells the true life story of an important person?

| | | | | | | | | |
|---|---|---|---|---|---|---|---|---|

58  12  16  48  66  30  69  50  53

**8** What is the golf term for a light tap that rolls the ball along the ground?

| | | | |
|---|---|---|---|

39  55  10  33

**9** Which is the only US state named after a president?

| | | | | | | | | | |
|---|---|---|---|---|---|---|---|---|---|

49  17  15  11  71  23  14  1  35  8

**10** Seven years after the invention of the telephone, what now-common greeting appeared in the dictionary for the first time?

29 37 44 40 54

**12** A popular tourist attraction in Minnesota is a five-ton ball, 12 feet in diameter, made of what material?

64 34 46 72 5

**11** Only four months of the year have this number of days. What is the number?

70 2 62 56 42 61

## Mark Twain said:

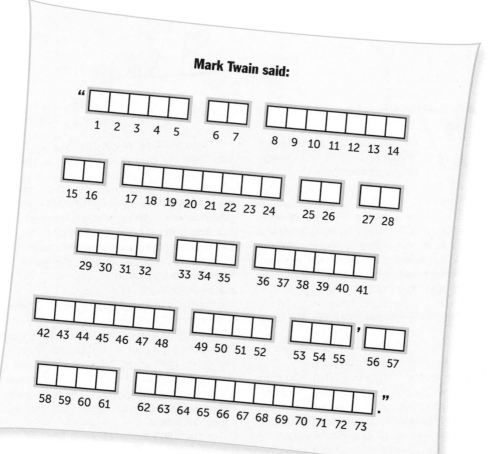

"[1 2 3 4 5] [6 7] [8 9 10 11 12 13 14]

[15 16] [17 18 19 20 21 22 23 24] [25 26] [27 28]

[29 30 31 32] [33 34 35] [36 37 38 39 40 41]

[42 43 44 45 46 47 48] [49 50 51 52] [53 54 55]'[56 57]

[58 59 60 61] [62 63 64 65 66 67 68 69 70 71 72 73]."

151

# Q: WHAT DO YOU CALL THE HISTORY OF THE RIDDLE?

## A: A BUNCH OF OLD JOKES

**W**hat do you call a misleading question with a surprisingly logical answer?

Give up? A *riddle*.

There's an ancient legend about a famous riddle asked by a sphinx—a mythical creature often depicted with a human's head and a lion's body. According to the legend, the sphinx used to guard the entrance to a Greek city. Before travelers could enter, they would have to answer a riddle:

*Which creature walks on four legs in the morning, two legs in the afternoon, and three legs in the evening?*

Talk about pressure—the sphinx would eat anyone who couldn't solve it!

The legend continues that Oedipus answered "Man" and was allowed to enter. *Man?* A man does not walk on four legs in the morning, two legs in the afternoon, and three legs in the evening. He only *has* two legs!

That's because you're thinking too *literally*. Think like a riddle solver and it all makes perfect sense: If you describe a person's whole lifetime as a single day, then morning is when you're a baby, afternoon is when you're an adult, and evening is when you're old. Babies crawl on all fours, adults walk on two legs, and old people walk with a cane.

Like most good riddles, the question seems impossible to answer, but the solution makes sense in a surprising way.

Riddles take many familiar forms. There's a common riddle type with a long history that compares two dissimilar things, with the answer being a pun of some kind. A riddle printed in 1833 asked, "How is a cold like a division in Congress?" The answer: "Because sometimes the eyes have it, and sometimes the nose." The pun is on "ayes" (yes votes) and "noes" (no votes).

In the 1865 book *Alice's Adventures in*

*Wonderland*, the Mad Hatter asks one of these comparison riddles:

*Why is a raven like a writing desk?*

When Alice gives up, the Hatter admits that he doesn't have the slightest idea either. In fact, Lewis Carroll, the book's author, originally intended this to be a riddle without a solution. But so many readers wrote to him asking for the answer that for a later edition he thought up a few possible solutions, including these:

- *Because it can produce a few notes, though they are very flat.*
- *Because it is nevar put with the wrong end in front!*

You may have noticed that in the second answer Carroll seems to have spelled the word *never* wrong. But in fact, he is saying "It is 'raven' spelled backwards" ("nevar" with the wrong end in front).

Perhaps one of the most familiar riddles of all goes like this:

*Why did the chicken cross the road?*

The answer is, "To get to the other side." It's rather strange that this has become one of the most well-known riddles, because although it *sounds* like a riddle, it is actually more like an "anti-riddle." It seems like the answer will be a chicken-y pun about eggs, or feathers, or hens. But the real answer is that the chicken crossed the road for the same not-funny reason that anybody or anything crosses a road. Believe it or not, this riddle first appeared in print in 1847.

**An even older style of riddle took a familiar concept and described it in an unfamiliar or misleading way. The object was to figure out what was being described. Try this one, which was written in the 1700s in the form of a rhyme:**

> *Before my birth I had a name,*
> *But soon as born I chang'd the same;*
> *And when I'm laid within the tomb,*
> *I shall my father's name assume.*
> *I change my name three days together*
> *Yet live but one in any weather.*

Very mysterious. Who could it be? Well, for starters, it's not a "who," it's a "what." Let's look at each part:

> *Before my birth I had a name,*
> *But soon as born I chang'd the same;*

(Before I come into existence I'm called one thing, but I'm called something else as soon as I arrive.)

> *And when I'm laid within the tomb,*
> *I shall my father's name assume.*

(And when I'm done, I'm given the same name as the one that came before me.)

> *I change my name three days together*
> *Yet live but one in any weather.*

(I change my name three days in a row, but I'm only one day long.)

**Can you figure out what's being described?**

For a puzzle with a Knock-Knock joke, see Someone's Knocking.

 **THE PUZZLE**

Each object in the top row can become an item in the bottom row if an R is added to its name. Use a ruler to connect the dots next to the pictures that go together. Each line you draw will eliminate the word in any circle you pass through, even if the line doesn't go through the word itself. When you're done, the words in the remaining circles will reveal a riddle. Write each of the four words *with the added Rs* in the boxes along the bottom, in the order of the shorter, numbered words. The highlighted boxes will spell the riddle's answer.

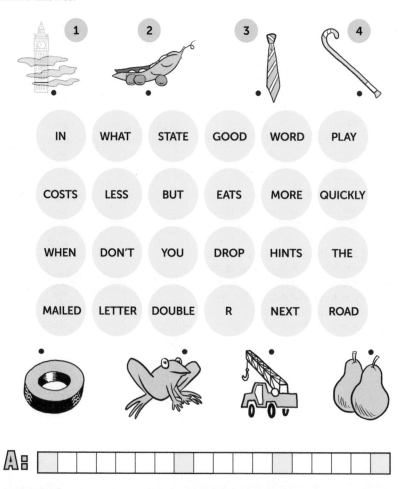

# RAIN CHECK

There's rain in the forecast, and it's your job to find where the raindrops will appear. The total number of hidden drops is shown below each grid. The numbers at the top and side of each grid tell you how many drops are in that row or column. In addition, each umbrella's tip points directly toward a raindrop—but the raindrop could be right next to the umbrella or far away! And not every raindrop will have an umbrella pointing to it. You'll find it useful to know where a raindrop *can't* be, so if you know a space must be empty, mark it with an X.

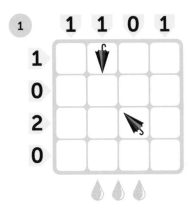

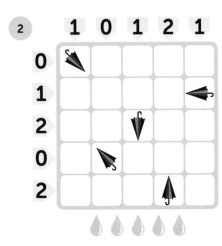

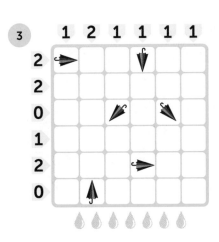

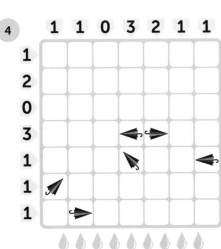

# RE-PAIR SHOP

First, identify the items below. Then fill those words into the two columns in the only boxes they'll fit in, placing the words from the left-hand set of pictures on the left and the words from the right-hand set on the right. The shaded boxes (which go across the columns) will spell a series of words that have something in common. Can you figure out what it is? (For a hint, look at this puzzle's title.)

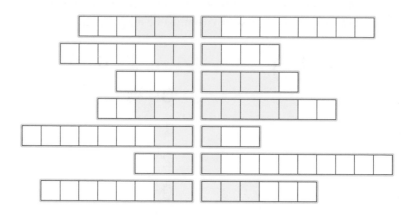

A⋮ _____

# RETURN TRIPS

The words that complete the blanks in each of these sentences are in reverse order of each other, such as LIAR and RAIL. Can you fill in all the pairs?

**1** When my teacher told me to remove my chewing _____ , I stuck it on the side of her coffee _____ .

**2** The sign on the door said " _____ out!" but I took a _____ when no one was watching.

**3** Since I was so worried about getting an electrical shock, I took a big _____ before I pulled the _____ out of the wall.

**4** The tailor secured my hem with _____ , then picked up scissors and began to _____ away the extra material.

**5** Last Halloween I dressed up as a _____ , and the kid who _____ next door dressed up as an angel.

**6** My grandmother hand-dyes the yarn that she _____ mittens with, but when the mittens get wet, they _____ like rotten eggs.

**7** The tool set has lots of loose _____ , but it comes packaged in a case with a _____ you can put over your shoulder.

**8** My parents _____ the babysitter the money she spent on an emergency _____ she used to change my baby brother.

**9** When my dad discovered that his wallet was not in his dresser _____ , he offered a _____ of five dollars to whoever found it.

**10** The hostess looked very _____ out when she realized that everyone ate so much at dinner that no one had room for the many delicious-looking _____ she had baked.

# REVOLUTIONARY IDEA

To find the answer to the riddle, start by identifying the seven pictures shown here. Then fit those words into the boxes below. Each answer word is a different length, so there is only one way to place each answer. When you're done, the circled letters will reveal the riddle's answer.

**Q:** Why was the invention of the drill such a big deal?

**A:** _____

# RHYME SPREE

Everything pictured here rhymes with its neighbor. For example, the QUILL rhymes with the bird's BILL. But look again—the bill can also be identified as a BEAK, which rhymes with a word describing the next picture. Continue following the path, identifying every picture with two different words (except the QUILL and the picture at the bottom right) in order to complete the puzzle.

159

# RHYMING SLANG

## THAT'S USING YOUR LOAF!

One of the liveliest forms of slang is *rhyming slang*, often known as *Cockney rhyming slang* because of how commonly it is used in East London, the home of the Cockney accent ("'Ello, guv'nah!").

Rhyming slang takes an ordinary word (for example, "phone") and replaces it with something else entirely ("dog," in this case) . . . by using rhyming. The rhyming word is then usually removed. In this case, the rhyming word is "bone," which rhymes with "phone" but suggests the dog. Got that?

Another example is the word "head," which was first changed to a phrase that rhymes with it: "loaf of bread." The rhyming part was then removed, leaving "loaf" as the new word for "head." To this day, people in East London will commonly say "Use your loaf!" to mean "Think about it!"

Similarly, "look" became "butcher's hook" and then shortened to "butcher's." "Eyes" became "mince pies" (English fruit pies) and then finally just "minces." You can use your minces to have a butcher's.

"Stink" became "pen and ink" and then just "pen." You get the idea.

Cockney rhyming slang has even shown up in the United States. It's believed that "bread," American slang for money, came from the rhyming slang "bread and honey."

Although it dates back to the early 1800s, rhyming slang continues to be invented and used today. As London prepared to welcome visitors from around the world when it hosted the 2012 Olympic Games, Cockney rhyming slang was offered as one of five language options at bank machines in East London. Buttons on the screen told customers to enter their "Huckleberry Finn" (instead of their "PIN," or personal identification number) in order to withdraw "sausage and mash" (cash), such as a "speckled hen" (a "ten"). It's enough to make a visitor's loaf spin.

Did you ever wonder why the rude sound you make when you blow air out around your lips and tongue is called a "raspberry"? It comes from rhyming slang. The original substituted phrase was "raspberry tart" and "tart" rhymes with . . . what?

# RIPPLE PLAY

Floating around in this grid are the names of places where you can find water. The words read left, right, up, down, and diagonally. When you've found them all, read the leftover letters (from left to right, top to bottom) to get an Interesting Fact.

```
E  E  C  L  L  E  W  G  N  I  H  S  I  W  U  T
D  C  S  N  P  B  U  C  K  E  T  Q  I  U  M  E
I  B  P  O  R  A  I  N  C  L  O  U  D  S  E  A
R  R  O  O  H  T  L  A  N  A  C  I  S  A  A  P
E  L  N  G  R  H  E  A  Q  U  A  R  I  U  M  O
M  N  G  A  I  T  N  E  K  T  S  T  E  Y  C  T
U  O  E  L  P  U  D  D  L  E  I  G  S  E  I  X
L  P  A  E  R  B  C  E  N  T  N  U  A  W  K  A
F  T  H  T  O  O  B  G  N  I  K  N  U  D  E  R
```

| | | |
|---|---|---|
| AQUARIUM | HOSE | PUDDLE |
| BATHTUB | LAGOON | RAIN CLOUD |
| BUCKET | LAKE | SINK |
| CANAL | MOAT | SPONGE |
| CREEK | OASIS | SQUIRT GUN |
| DUNKING BOOTH | OCEAN | TEAPOT |
| FLUME RIDE | POOL | WISHING WELL |

## INTERESTING FACT:

__ __ __ __ __ __ __ __ __   __ __

__ __ __ __ __ __ - __ __ __

__ __ __ __ __ __ __ __   __ __ __ __ __ .

161

# ROCKET RACKET

In this story, 19 pairs of words have been replaced with numbered blanks. The words in each pair are identical except for a single vowel, which has been changed to a different vowel. When you come to a blank, find its numbered mate to help you figure out both missing words. Pair #1 has been filled in to get you started.

A 1 ___ROCKET___ carrying three astronauts was launched one morning at the break of 2 _____.
The mission would take eleven years—more than a complete 3 _____—to get to Mars, collect a soil 4 _____, and bring it home.

The first day, one astronaut offered to spend time 5 _____ the angles and speeds they would need to safely touch 2 _____ on the surface of the 6 _____ planet.

" 7 _____ you for offering, but you'd 8 _____ let me do it," said the second astronaut. "I'm kind of a 9 _____ at math, if I do say so myself. I'll do it tonight, 10 _____ you're both catching 11 _____ ZZZ's."

The third astronaut laughed at the others. "You 12 _____ be joking. I could probably get more brain power from a 13 _____ of coal."

The first astronaut clenched her 14 _____ and said, "Oh, are we 5 _____ against each other for the title of '12 _____ Obnoxious Astronaut'? Congratulations, you both win!"

From then on, the astronauts annoyed each other like three

162

9 _____ stuck in the 11 _____ 13 _____ .
They made a terrible 1 ___RACKET___ with their constant arguing. And they
often 15 _____ up their daily routines because they were distracted,
putting the timeline of the 10 _____ mission in jeopardy.

Now they would have to gather the soil quickly and not 16 _____ on
Mars even a minute 16 _____ than necessary. There would be no time
for 17 _____ aimlessly from crater to crater.

One day, the head of the mission came over the intercom
and said, "We know you can't wait to be
6 _____ of each other, but we were
17 _____ if we could interrupt.
We have something to say that we
7 _____ will put an end
to your 8 _____ feud."

"Make it 14 _____ ,
because we're busy," one of the
astronauts replied. "We're trying
to 3 _____ whose
foot will take the historic first
18 _____ onto the surface."

"This will make it very
4 _____ ," came the
voice. "19 _____ of you
will go first. After six years,
19 _____ months, and
three days of arguing, you just
15 _____ your
18 _____ !"

# ROUNDUP

At the center of this puzzle is a riddle. To find the answer, start by solving the clues around it. Spell out each answer starting in the nearest circle with an arrow and working your way around the clue in the direction indicated by the arrow. When you're done, the letters that surround the riddle will spell the answer. The answer's starting letter and direction are for you to determine.

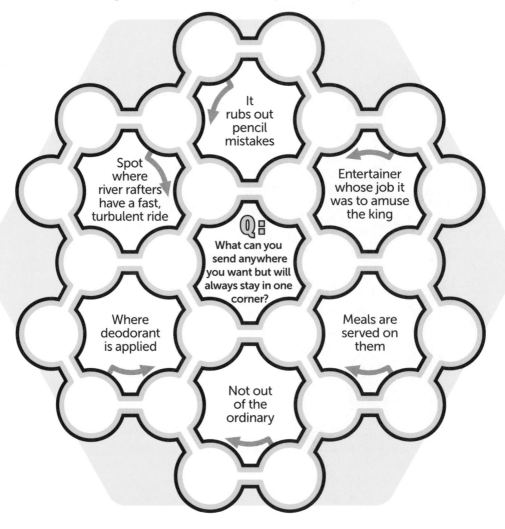

It rubs out pencil mistakes

Spot where river rafters have a fast, turbulent ride

Entertainer whose job it was to amuse the king

**Q:** What can you send anywhere you want but will always stay in one corner?

Where deodorant is applied

Meals are served on them

Not out of the ordinary

**A:** _ _ _ _ _ _ _

# RUSH HOUR

The panels in this comic strip are shown out of order. Number the blank circles with the correct order so the strip tells a funny story.

# THE PUZZLE

This puzzle has two parts. First, read the clues and fill in the answers. When you're done, cross out pairs of answers that are identical except for whether the S is at the beginning or the end. For example, you would cross out STACK and TACKS. Three words will remain. Move their Ss to the other end to get three words that have something in common. Write the new words and their common theme on the lines at the end.

**1** Moves along the floor like a baby
___ ___ ___ ___ ___

**2** Stretch a muscle beyond its normal limit
___ ___ ___ ___ ___

**3** Hammers hit them
___ ___ ___ ___ ___

**4** Weapon for Hercules or King Arthur
___ ___ ___ ___ ___

**5** Mess made by splashing sauce
___ ___ ___ ___ ___ ___ ___

**6** Parts that planes, birds, and butterflies have in common
___ ___ ___ ___ ___

**7** Sloppy, hard-to-read handwriting
___ ___ ___ ___ ___

**8** Animal that leaves a trail of slime
___ ___ ___ ___ ___

**9** Big serving dishes
___ ___ ___ ___ ___ ___

**10** _____ by lightning
___ ___ ___ ___ ___

**11** Contents of a dictionary
___ ___ ___ ___ ___

**12** Permanent mark on your body after a wound heals
___ ___ ___ ___

**13** Try to hit a baseball
___ ___ ___ ___ ___

_____

_____

_____

**COMMON THEME:**
_____

166

# SAND-WHICH

Uh-oh—quicksand will soon cover up these words, each of which can come after SAND to form a word or phrase like SANDPIT or SANDBLASTER. Can you figure out each word from the small amount that remains?

CASTLE

TRAP

DUNE

DOLLAR

BAGS

STORM

PAPER

CRAB

BOX

# PUZZLE BREAKERS

## SAY WHAT?

### THE STRANGE ORIGINS OF FAMILIAR PHRASES

**W**hy do we say "it's raining cats and dogs" when it's pouring out? Why do theater people say "Break a leg" to wish each other good luck? In these and many other cases, nobody is entirely sure where these colorful expressions, called *idioms*, came from. But for the seven phrases listed below, the origins are known, and now it's time to "spill the beans." For each idiom, there are two stories given about its origin. One is real, but one is made up. Can you tell which is which?

**1** **SPEAKING OFF THE CUFF**
(speaking without preparation)

a In England, people on trial could remove their handcuffs in court. It was believed that cuffs made them look guilty before they had a chance to defend themselves.

b People who did not have time to carefully prepare a speech would jot down a few notes on their shirt cuff with a pencil. They could then appear to be speaking spontaneously, when in fact they were reading notes off their cuff.

**2** **CLOSE, BUT NO CIGAR** (not quite)

a During World War II, when British prime minister Winston Churchill took ill, his staff hired a look-alike to show up at public events and wave to the crowd. This worked until a keen-eyed reporter photographed the impostor smoking a cigarette—something the cigar-smoking Churchill would never do. The next day's headline, "Close, But No Cigar," gave us the phrase we use today.

b Carnivals and fairs would sometimes offer cigars as prizes in games like ring toss. Players who played well but lost were often told "Close, but no cigar."

**3** **WILD-GOOSE CHASE**
(a lot of effort that will probably be pointless)

a The original "wild-goose chase" was actually a kind of horse race in which the leading rider would allow his horse to run wildly and the other riders would follow like a flock of geese. After Shakespeare used the phrase, it became a permanent part of the language.

b    At village festivals it was common to offer a large prize to anyone who would get in a pen and catch a wild goose by the feet. Not surprisingly, it is nearly impossible to catch a wild goose, so the prize was never won. Today the expression is used for any exhausting effort that is bound to end in disappointment.

**4    THROW IN THE TOWEL** (give up)

a    When a boxer was losing a fight very badly, his manager would signal that the bout should end by throwing the boxer's towel into the middle of the ring.

b    Merchants tried to lure in customers during the Great Depression by giving away free dish towels when people bought something. When shoppers argued for a better price, they knew they'd won the negotiation when the business owner gave up and "threw in" the free towel.

**5    EASY AS PIE** (very easy)

a    This phrase refers to how pleasant and easy it is to *eat* pie, not to bake it. In the 1880s, people were described as "polite as pie" and easy tasks were "like eating pie." Over time the phrase became simply "easy as pie."

b    The phrase began as "easy-peasy" and then became "easy as pieces of cake." During the Civil War, Southerners adopted the first half, "easy as pie," while Northerners took the second half, "piece of cake." Today both phrases are common and have the same meaning.

**6    FLY OFF THE HANDLE** (have an uncontrolled outburst)

a    During warm months, flies would gather near American settlers' food. The cook would "shoo" the flies off the handles of pots and pans, but they would simply buzz around crazily for a moment and land right back where they started.

b    American pioneers would attach steel axe heads to handles they had whittled themselves. Occasionally the axe head became loose and flew off midswing, causing damage (or injury!). Eventually an out-of-control person was said to "fly off the handle" the way the axe heads did.

**7    THINK OUTSIDE THE BOX** (think creatively)

a    This phrase came from a puzzle in which the challenge was to draw lines through a square grid of dots. The surprise solution involved drawing some of the lines beyond the square's edges. The popular puzzle proved that sometimes to get the answer, you have to think "outside the box."

b    The box refers to a business office. A successful business leader coined this phrase to suggest that employees who keep coming up with the same ideas should look for solutions from outside the office.

# SIDEWINDERS

In each Sidewinder maze, find one continuous path from START to FINISH that goes through every box except the ones with snakes. You may go through each box only once, and your path may not cross itself. The mazes get harder as you progress—be sure to use a pencil with a good eraser! There is only one way to solve each maze.

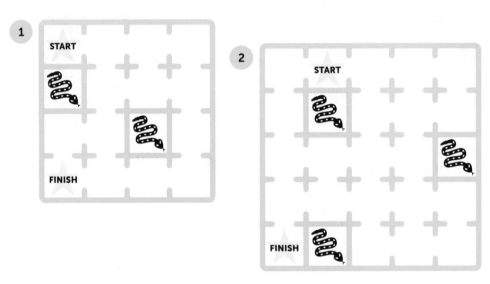

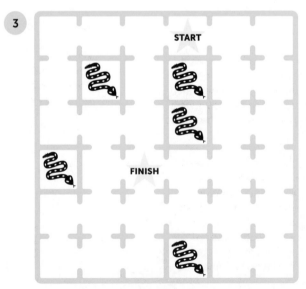

170

# SOMEONE'S KNOCKING

Knock, knock. *Who's there?* Doris. *Doris who?* That's for you to figure out. Read each clue and write your answers in the blanks. Every answer will contain either the letters L-O-C-K or K-E-Y, always together in a chunk (like "bLOCKbuster" or "KEY West"). When you're done, read down one column to get the rest of Doris's name.

| # | Clue |
|---|------|
| 1 | _____ and the Three Bears |
| 2 | Game played on ice with a puck |
| 3 | Disney World's most famous mouse |
| 4 | This announces the hour with a bird that springs out of a door |
| 5 | Where athletes put on their uniforms |
| 6 | Long-eared animal that hee-haws |
| 7 | This protects your skin at the beach |
| 8 | Person who rides a racehorse |
| 9 | Shepherd's group of sheep |
| 10 | Where your fingers go, either on a piano or a computer |
| 11 | Thanksgiving bird |
| 12 | Chimp |
| 13 | Detective with the last name Holmes |
| 14 | You hold this down to type a capital letter |
| 15 | Mesh together, like gears |

A🔒 Doris _____ !

# SPEED LIMIT

The sign on this winding road says 15 MPH, but before you step on the brakes, look again. There are 15 things in this town that can be described using the initials M-P-H. For example, if a wealthy person was stuffing hammers into luggage, that would be a Millionaire Packing Hammers. Can you get them all without slowing down?

VACANCY

A CYCLONE WILL HIT NEXT YEAR

# SPIN CYCLE

The names of things that spin are written in order around these circles. It's up to you to figure out where each word begins and whether it goes clockwise or counterclockwise around the circle. Can you get them all?

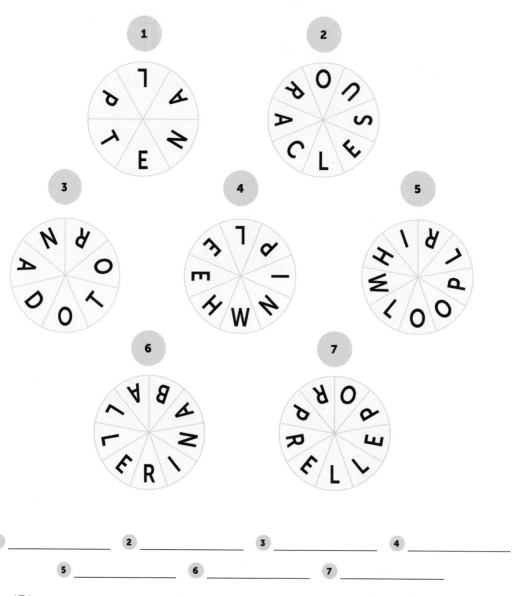

1 _____   2 _____   3 _____   4 _____

5 _____   6 _____   7 _____

# SPLIT DECISION

To find the answer to the riddle, use the clues to fill in the words in the spaces provided. Each word is split into two halves. The arrow in each clue tells you in which direction the second half of your answer should go. When you're done, the highlighted letters in order, from top to bottom, will answer the riddle.

**Q:** **What items get heavier after they are broken into pieces?**

1 ↘ The type of question at the start of this puzzle

2 ↗ Curly-haired dog
2 ↘ Completely exhausted

3 ↗ Said "thothage" instead of "sausage," for example
3 ↘ Pay attention to what's being said

4 ↗ Like red-hot lava
4 ↘ Back teeth

5 ↗ Takes an oath
5 ↘ Turn abruptly to avoid driving into something

6 ↗ Go without eating
6 ↘ Home for horses

7 ↗ Possible to eat
7 ↘ Inventor of the light bulb

8 ↗ President whose first name was Woodrow
8 ↘ Tree that might be "weeping"

9 ↗ Item at the head of a bed
9 ↘ They fly planes

**A:** _____

# PUZZLE BREAKERS
# SPOONERISMS
## ROARING PAIN AND POURING RAIN

**B**efore you read about spoonerisms, you might want to find yourself a nosy little cook. If you already realize that the correct phrase is "a cozy little nook," then you're good at spotting spoonerisms.

*Spoonerisms* are named after William Archibald Spooner, who, despite being a respected lecturer at Oxford University in England, was famous for mixing up his words—usually switching the beginnings of two words. For example, he once supposedly said that someone had been killed by "a blushing crow" instead of "a crushing blow." Supposedly he also told a lazy student that he had "tasted a whole worm." What he meant to say was that the student had "wasted a whole term."

Accidental spoonerisms can happen to anyone from time to time, although they usually result in nonsense (such as saying "One swell foop" instead of "one fell swoop"). But other times, the switch results in a real-sounding phrase. Here are some memorable examples:

save the whales / wave the sails

taking a shower / shaking a tower

a half-formed wish / a half-warmed fish

carrots and peas / parrots and keys

Not all spoonerisms involve switching the beginnings of words. During a 1931 radio broadcast in honor of president Herbert Hoover's birthday, the announcer accidentally switched his middles, referring to the president as "Hoobert Heever."

Writer and illustrator Shel Silverstein's book *Runny Babbit* is filled with spoonerisms. Throughout it, the beginning sounds of words are switched, but they don't usually make new words—just nonsense that's fun to say. (Silverstein called it "a billy sook.")

For much of Spooner's life he denied that he had made most of these mistakes. However, as he got older, he stopped complaining, and even allowed spoonerisms to be attributed to him that he never really said. Would you call that going back on your word?

Or going whack on your bird?

---

Here are clues for phrases that are spoonerisms of each other. Can you figure out what they are? For example, "Battling people who don't tell the truth / Burning things down" would be "Fighting liars" and "Lighting fires."

1. Crying geckos and iguanas / Jumping Hogwarts students
2. Place to buy quacking birds / Entranceway that is hard to open
3. What a rabbit uses to make a call / Part of the elbow that tingles painfully if it gets banged

*For some other groan-worthy puzzles, see Didja Ever See . . .? and Naming Names.*

# SWEET TALK

Cutting down on sweets has gone too far! Some of the candy pieces that make the letters in each of the sweets listed here have been removed. The whole alphabet is shown below to help you see what's missing. Can you get them all?

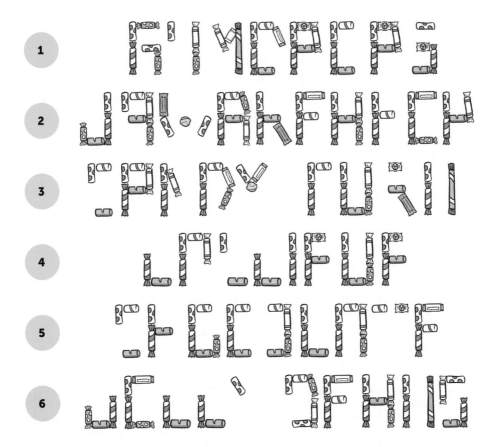

# THE PUZZLE

THERE'S **NOTHING GOOD** ON THIS MENU!

YES, BUT...

Two termites took turns talking. But what is the second one saying? To find out, read the twelve clues. The answer to each is a two-word phrase in which both words start with T (like *topsy turvy*). Cross off each word in the list below as you use it. When you're done, four words will remain. Put them in order from shortest to longest to complete the termite's response.

1  A fit of crying and screaming by an out-of-control child

2  An amazing amount of things found all at once

3  Another name for a seesaw

4  Person who allows you to enter a theater or stadium

5  Phrase like "She sells seashells by the seashore"

6  Place where vacationers are stuck overpaying for everything

7  Outlandish story

8  Science-fiction theory that lets people visit the future or the past

9  The very best items in a ranked list

10  Thin glass container used by scientists

11  Vehicle that removes broken-down cars from the road

12  What lumber is made from

| TASTES | TALL | TREASURE | TAKER | TRAVEL |
|--------|------|----------|-------|--------|
| TREE | TWISTER | TERRIFIC | TOURIST | TANTRUM |
| TEST | TOP | TRUCK | TABLE | TEN |
| TEETER | TIME | TEMPER | TRUNKS | TALE |
| TUBE | THIS | TONGUE | TOTTER | TROVE |
| | TRAP | TICKET | TOW | |

**A:** "Yes, but _____ _____ _____ _____!"

# TASTE-MAKERS

Fill in each row of boxes with the name of one of the objects shown here. Some letters have been placed to get you started. When you've filled every box, the two shaded columns, reading down, will spell the answer to the riddle.

**Q:** What should you put in soup to make its flavor richer?

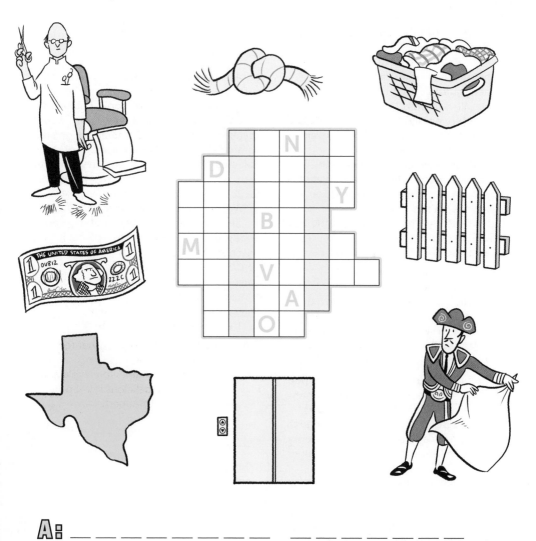

**A:** _ _ _ _ _ _ _   _ _ _ _ _ _

# PUZZLE BREAKERS

# TOM FOOLERY

**TOM SWIFTIES**

"This page is about Tom Swifties," said Tom.

"Never heard of them," said Harry.

"They're funny," said Tom.

"Then I guess I'll like them," said Harry.

"You will," said Tom.

Sound boring? All Tom and Harry do is "say" stuff. Wouldn't it be better if Tom "explained" or "uttered" or even "said helpfully"?

Tom Swifties are funny. In a Tom Swifty, Tom says something, but it's *how* he says it that's the funny part. A pun is hidden there, commenting on what he's just said. For example:

"Looks like we'll have to walk all the way there," Tom said tirelessly.

Get it? No tires. That's why they'll have to walk.

Here are a few more:

- "If I get any taller, that ceiling fan may lop my head off!" Tom said gruesomely.
- "Oh yeah! I've decided to stay in the club for another year," Tom remembered.
- "I come from Kansas," Tom stated flatly.

The fun part is looking for the hidden pun. Tom said "gruesomely" because he grew some. (You can figure out the other two.)

All of these sentences sound as though they come from a story, but there is no story. There's only Tom and his funny—or rather, punny—way of saying things.

At this point you may be wondering, "Who is Tom Swifty?" Actually, there once were Tom Swift stories. The name comes from a series of books about a young scientist named Tom Swift who invents futuristic things like rocket ships and ray guns. These books started in the 1910s and more than 100 have been published over many decades.

The authors of these books had a habit of colorfully describing how Tom would speak. For example: "'Come along!' invited Tom cordially" or "'I don't want to do that,' objected Tom." It could become tiring to read after a while. Since Tom's name was Swift, an early Tom Swift joke went like this:

"We must hurry," said Tom *swiftly*.

See, his name is Swift, but he spoke *swiftly*, because he's . . . okay, you get it.

From there, other writers decided to put Tom into new situations and describe punny ways for him to speak. Maybe these puns should be known as Tom "Swiftlies," but the name "Tom Swifties" stuck instead.

Here are a few more favorites:

- "I will not drown in Egypt!" shouted Tom, deep in denial.
- "I just got off my flight," Tom explained.
- "This is the most delicious salmon I'll ever eat," said Tom superficially.

---

**Can you fill in the two words that complete this Tom Swifty?**

"The exit is right there," Tom

p __ __ __ __ __ __ __ __

o __ __ __ __ __ .

# TRACKING DOWN

To get from HIDE to SEEK, answer each clue with a word that's just one letter different from the word before it. If you can't find your way down, try solving from the bottom up.

**H I D E**

This part of the cube

A historically polite term of address for this person

How this person's muscle feels

This part of a shoe

What this person is known for sliding down

A heap like this

Tree that produces objects like this

Color of ice cream flavored like this fruit

Plastic item sometimes used to play this instrument

This movement by a hen

What this person may do between his fingers

**S E E K**

# TYPE CASTING

Each line of text on the next page forms a miniature scene in which one of the "characters" is speaking. Match each caption at the bottom of this page with the word balloon in a picture on the right that helps the picture make sense. Hint: Start by thinking about the setting suggested by each caption. Then ignore what the letters and symbols mean, and concentrate on what they look like. In the example below, the single "i" is a person looking into a crowded elevator. (See the brackets that are the elevators doors? See the little UP light?)

**EXAMPLE:** "Never mind—I'll take the stairs."

a   "Stuart, keep your eyes on your own paper!"

b   "See, son? There in the thicket! A baby giraffe!"

c   "I don't know . . . I just don't have that school spirit."

d   "Isn't that cute! A bicycle built for two!"

e   "Eddie, in my gym class nobody is excused from jumping jacks."

f   "All right, break it up! No fighting!"

g   "I told you not to lean against the Greek ruins!"

h   "Am I too late for the hula hoop competition?"

i   "I always see the same hands, class. Anyone else?"

j   "Shut the window—the snow is starting to blow in!"

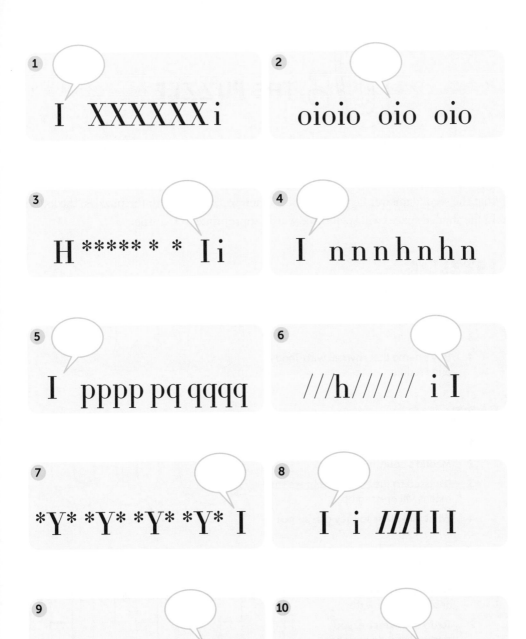

 **THE PUZZLE**

In each of these puzzles of U-turns, fill in the five-letter answer to each clue in the U that matches the clue's number, starting at the top left and continuing around to the top right. In the first puzzle, TURNS has been filled in to get you started, which shows that the second answer begins with SN. When you're done with the puzzles, the letters in the shaded spaces will spell three words appropriate to U-turns.

## PUZZLE A

1   Makes a left, a right, or a U
2   Noise from the nose of a pig or horse
3   Swap
4   Boy's name that rhymes with Teddy and Freddie

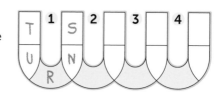

## PUZZLE B

1   Lends a hand
2   Madrid's country
3   "Dressed to the _____" (phrase that means "all dressed up")
4   What you plant so they can sprout

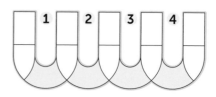

## PUZZLE C

1   Small refreshing area in a desert that has water
2   To do this exercise, you start by lying on your back
3   Closer to being 100% uncontaminated
4   Fishing equipment rods and _____
5   Nightly rest
6   Flower piece removed when you say "He loves me"

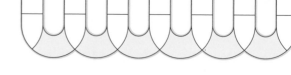

# UDDER CONFUSION

Time to play a little cowhide and seek. Each of the five numbered cows has three spots shaped like objects in a common category. And each of the five spots on the fenced-in cow at the bottom can also fit one of the categories. Figure out the category for each numbered cow, and determine which one of the spots from the bottom cow belongs with it.

# UNDERCOVER ASSIGNMENT

Urgent message to all agents: Your mission is to search this grid and find the spy-related words listed below. When you've completed your task, read the leftover letters (from left to right, top to bottom) to get a secret Bonus Message. You should then rip up this page and destroy the pieces!

```
        S  P  E  C
     C  A  S  E  A  G
  C  I  C  E  Y  M  S  U
S  R  A  L  U  C  O  N  I  B
H  P  L  M  R  E  U  C  L  P
E  F  I  L  E  S  F  E  E  D
M  D  A  G  P  R  L  E  I  D
   I  S  O  O  R  A  S  G
      S  E  R  W  G  A
         S  T  U  E
         S  I  S  H
      S  S  N  O  O  P
      E  I  N  E  N  G
      S  T  G  M  A  T
      S  E  A  O  N  K
   D  A  P  D  E  N  S  Y
   A  L  D  G  O  C  H  E
   N  G  A  E  I  C  A  F
   G  K  E  T  A  T  D  T
T  E  R  C  E  S  P  O  T  H
E  R  A  B  R  I  T  W  I  S
H  T  D  R  O  W  S  S  A  P
```

AGENT
ALIAS
BINOCULARS
BUG
CAMERA
CAMOUFLAGE
CASE
CODE
DANGER
DARK GLASSES
DECOY
DISGUISE
ESCAPE
FILES
GADGET
MAP
MISSION
PASSWORD
REPORT
SHADOWS
SNEAKY
SNOOP
TACTICS
TOP SECRET

# BONUS MESSAGE:

_____ _____  _____ _____

_____ _____ _____ _____

___ _____ .

186

# UNITED NATIONS

Each of these sentences has the name of a single country hidden somewhere inside, across two or more words. For example, in the first sentence, SPAIN appears in IT'S PAINFUL. How many of them can you find?

**1** After all that walking today, it's painful for me to stand up at all.

**2** Even if you've seen a zebra zillions of times in the zoo, there's nothing like seeing one in the wild.

**3** I know how eager many people would be to travel to Europe, but I'd rather spend my vacation relaxing at home.

**4** During the Halloween dance, one person dressed as a ninja panted so loudly that I was afraid he'd collapse.

**5** The planetarium had exhibits about each strategy Ptolemy used to study the heavens.

**6** We don't drink soda at home, but when we're on vacation we're each allowed one can a day.

**7** Along with taking a lot of photographs, my mom likes to record our trips in diaries.

**8** Dad said the choice was ours: Pack light for our trip or tug a lot of luggage behind us everywhere we went.

**9** Most of the shady spots at the outdoor festival were either already taken or way too far from the stage.

**10** Our excellent tour guide took us to a lovely hidden marketplace that tourists don't usually get to see.

**11** We looked up an amazing art museum that I'd like to visit when we're in the capital.

**12** I would have eaten lunch in any of the restaurants we walked past, but Dad insisted on finding the one he saw in the travel guide.

# UPS AND DOWNS

## LET'S LOOK AT AMBIGRAMS ANOTHER WAY

I f you print the word SWIMS in capital letters on a piece of paper, you can turn it upside down and it will still spell SWIMS.

If you hold the word MOM up to a mirror, it will still spell MOM. And if you write it out like this:

and hold a mirror vertically along the middle of the letters so that half of each letter is reflected in the mirror, it *still* spells MOM.

Those are ambigrams.

You might find yourself saying WOW— WOW is MOM upside down. That's an ambigram, too.

*Ambigrams* are designs that you can view in two different ways (*ambi* means "both" and *gram* is used for anything written). They take many forms: Some read the same in both directions, some change from one message into another, some go up and down, and others go side to side. They are some of the most interactive forms of wordplay because they often ask you to pick up the page and do something with it, like turning it or holding it up to a mirror. And while most involve words, some ambigrams are pictures.

puzzlelopedia

Take a look at PUZZLELOPEDIA, above. When you turn the word upside down, it says PUZZLELOPEDIA again. The L in the middle doesn't change, but everything else becomes something different when viewed the other way.

The same thing happens with UPSIDE DOWN, an ambigram by artist Scott Kim that's shown below. This one is even more interesting: somehow, the word UPSIDE becomes DOWN, and DOWN becomes UPSIDE.

The complete alphabet shown below, also by Scott Kim, was created to be a reflection of itself. He cleverly divided the letters into groups to help make this possible (such as by having P and Q face each other). But notice how part of the R becomes the complete S! This alphabet is full of little tricks like that, which work because our eyes automatically see it as the entire alphabet as soon as we look at it.

Not all ambigrams involve words. Over the years, artists have created logos, paintings, and even comic strips that play these sorts of tricks.

The panel below comes from a comic strip called *The Upside-Downs of Little Lady Lovekins and Old Man Muffaroo*. Readers of this comic strip, which ran in the *New York Herald* newspaper from 1903 to 1905, would read the first six panels in order, then turn the page upside down to see the last six panels of the story. In this case, it's the pictures themselves that change into new pictures.

Amazing, isn't it?

What word for a part of the day, when written in capital letters, reads the same when you hold it right side up and upside down?

 **THE PUZZLE**

This puzzle has two parts. First, follow the instructions about the words in the grid below and cross out one or more words per step. Look carefully to make sure you've got them all.

1. Cross out any word that can become a new word if V is added to the beginning.

2. Cross out any word that can become a new word if the first letter is changed to V.

3. Cross out any word that has the same meaning as the Roman numeral V.

4. Cross out any word that will spell the name of a number if the letter V is inserted somewhere inside it.

5. Cross out any word that can become a new word by changing a V to a U.

6. Cross out any word that is pronounced with a "V" sound even though it doesn't contain a V.

7. Cross out any word that becomes a new word if both Vs and all the letters between them are removed.

8. Cross out any word that has the same letters (in any order) before the first V and after the second V.

When you've crossed out all the words indicated in the instructions, there will be two words remaining. These two words, when viewed together, often take the shape of a V. What are those words?

| REVIVAL | VALVE | DIVISIVE |
|---------|-------|----------|
| CULTURE | ICE | REVOLVER |
| FLYING | SEEN | SURVIVE |
| ALLEY | LOCAL | GEESE |
| FIVE | OF | EASE |

# VAMPIRE BATCH

Only one of the silhouettes here has the same details as the flesh-and-blood picture in the middle. Can you tell which and spot the differences in the others?

# VARIETY SHOW

There are five acts in tonight's show: acrobatics, singing, juggling, magic, and a dog act. All the performers are waiting backstage for their turn in the spotlight. Use the clues below to figure out the order in which the acts will appear.

The dogs can't wait very long so they're going first or second.

A performer with a hat is going last.

Immediately after the juggler is an act with two people in it.

The dog act appears immediately before or after the magic act because they're sharing hoops.

The juggler and the magicians are fighting so they're not appearing immediately before or after each other.

**TONIGHT'S LINEUP**

1. _____
2. _____
3. _____
4. _____
5. _____

# VEG OUT

Hope you like your veggies chopped! Each clue leads to an answer of one or two words. Some of the letters in the answer are given. The letters that you write in the blanks will spell the name of a vegetable. Can you root them all out?

**1**   Maybe

☐ ☐ R H ☐ P ☐

**2**   Place where someone might be taken after being arrested

☐ ☐ L I C E   S ☐ ☐ ☐ I ☐ N

**3**   Squeezable musical instrument with a keyboard

A ☐ C ☐ D I O ☐

**4**   Movie star or other famous person

☐ ☐ ☐ ☐ B ☐ I T ☐

**5**   A common kind of pants made of denim

☐ L U ☐   J E ☐ ☐ ☐

**6**   Personal judgment

☐ P I ☐ ☐ ☐ ☐

**7**   Robot

A U ☐ ☐ ☐ ☐ ☐ N

**8**   Easily grossed out

☐ ☐ ☐ E ☐ M I ☐ ☐

**9**   Something that restores your energy

☐ ☐ I C K ☐ R - U ☐ ☐ ☐

# PUZZLE BREAKERS

# VISUAL TRICKERY
## AND OPTICAL ILLUSIONS

I f "seeing is believing," that's because we trust our eyes to make sense of what we're looking at. Buildings look smaller when they're far away, and long roads seem to come to a point as they go off into the distance. We don't bother thinking about these things, but just trust that they are so. Our brain puts these assumptions in the background so we can concentrate on the important stuff—like whether an animal in the distance is large (but far away) or not so large (but dangerously close).

Optical illusions show us that sometimes those assumptions can be wrong. The result is that our brain is tricked into seeing something it can't believe.

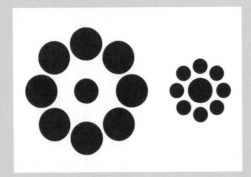

When you look at the two groups of dots above, for example, your brain instantly compares their sizes. Although the outer dots are different, the center dots are the same size as each other—promise! The one on the

left looks smaller because it's surrounded by big dots and a lot of blank space. The one on the right looks larger because it's crowded by small dots.

The illusion below takes advantage of how our eyes look for patterns. The horizontal lines separating these rows of tiles appear to be sloping up and down. But look again (and this time lay a ruler along the horizontal lines)! Not only are all the lines perfectly parallel, every square is, well, square. Because the columns aren't lined up, we're tricked into thinking that the horizontal lines are messed up, too.

At the top of the next page is one version of a classic "figure-ground" illusion. The black figure is a vase, which many people see as soon as they look at the image. But focus instead on the white "ground" (that is, the background) and think of the black vase shape as an empty background. Now you might see the two white faces in silhouette looking at each other. You may find it hard to see it both ways at the same time.

One aspect of visual trickery is so common that we never think of it at all: the way a flat drawing represents the three-dimensional world. In truth, an artist simply uses an understanding of perspective to arrange lines on a flat surface to give the illusion of space. When three-dimensional images are drawn in two dimensions, some sophisticated illusions can be introduced, as in this object:

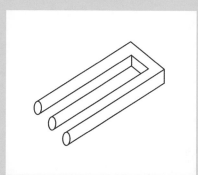

This item cannot be built in the "real world." It has three legs, but if you cover the legs you'll notice that the other end only has two branches. Also notice that the branches are square, but the ends are round!

Now look at the pictures on these two blocks. Believe it or not, the boy on the right is exactly the same as the one on the left—he has not been squashed at all. (Try tracing one, if you want to be convinced.) This illusion takes advantage of the fact that when three-dimensional objects are shown as flat drawings, our eyes assume that diagonal lines are moving off into the distance.

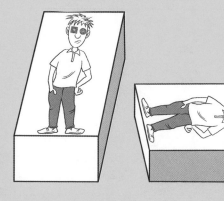

Here are four more objects that seem to be three-dimensional. Three of them are, in fact, impossible—they can't exist in three dimensions in real life, only on paper. One of them, though, shows a real, three-dimensional object. Can you tell which?

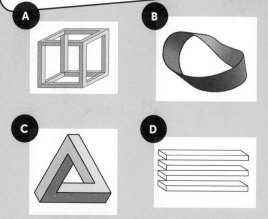

# VROOM SERVICE

This puzzle has two parts. First, connect the dots in order using a ruler. The path that you make will form the walls of a maze. Then solve the maze by drawing a path from the bell to the exhausted bellhop.

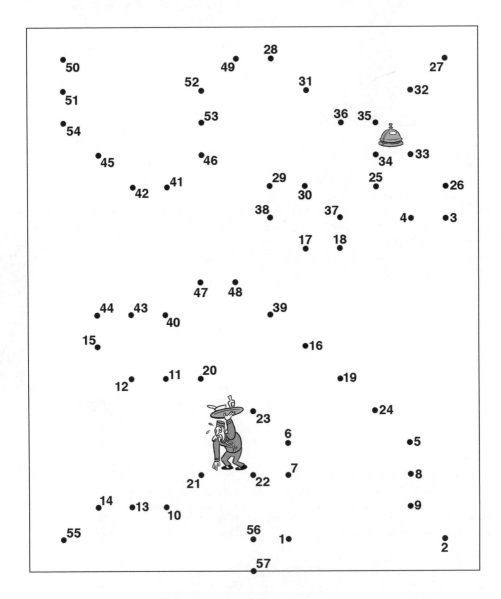

 **THE PUZZLE**

Every word here starts with W and has its own style of lettering—but the styles are not well matched to the words they spell. The word WEALTH, for example, would be more appropriately written in the style that says WRITER—because that looks like the lettering on money. Each word here can be matched with a different style on the page. Can you match them all?

# WAY TO GO!

The words and phrases listed below will fit into these boxes so that they interlock like a crossword puzzle. But everywhere the letters NORTH, SOUTH, EAST, or WEST appear together in the words, they have been replaced in the grid with an arrow pointing in that direction according to the compass. For example, if the phrase TELL ME A STORY were in the list, it would be entered in the grid as TELLM → ORY with an arrow replacing the consecutive letters E-A-S-T. Use the lengths of the words and the places where they cross as a guide to put them all in the correct spots. (Ignore punctuation and spaces between words.)

AWESTRUCK

BEAST OF BURDEN

BREASTSTROKE

DEEP SOUTH

EASTER EGG

GROSS-OUT HUMOR

LAST BUT NOT LEAST

MIDWEST

NEITHER HERE NOR THERE

NEWEST

NORTH POLE

NORTH STAR

SEA STAR

SLOWEST

SOUTH PARK

SOUTHWEST AIRLINES

TAKE A STAND

TEA STRAINER

UNITED WE STAND

UNORTHODOX

WILD WEST

# WEAVING A SPELL

The words in this web-shaped grid are arranged in two ways. Each INWARD clue leads to a five-letter word that you enter starting in the web space next to its numbered spider and continuing straight toward the web's center, one letter per space. The AROUND clues lead to words that read clockwise around the web's bands. Fill in those words starting in the numbered spaces in the web.

## INWARD

1  Haunted house inhabitant

2  Loses speed

3  Device in a submarine that sends out a pinging noise

4  Mustached plumber character in many Nintendo games

5  Rewrites or shortens a draft of a story

6  Item you bob for at a Halloween party

7  Kind of numerals on many grandfather clocks

8  Item put on an injured neck

9  Units for measuring land

## AROUND

1  Smudge

2  Containers for shoppers to carry items home in

3  Amount of clothes that can fit in the washer

4  Place you might stand when saying "Trick or treat!"

5  Tear apart, or letters found on a gravestone

6  Dark-red color

7  Be patient

8  Sneaker strings

9  Flower with thorns

10  Homes for birds

# WHAT'S THE BUZZ?

To solve the riddle, use the clues to fill in as many answer words as you can. The answers are the same both across and down, so enter them in both directions. When you've filled in all the words, use the symbols to transfer the letters to the boxes below to spell the riddle's answer.

**Q:** Why does it take so long to figure out where a mosquito has bitten you?

**1 2 3 4**

1 Make a sketch
2 Wealthy
3 Dull pain from a sore muscle
4 What Little Miss Muffet ate with her curds

1 Like a mattress you sink into
2 Woodwind instrument
3 Number of suits in a deck of cards
4 Division of the school year

**1 2 3 4**

**A:**

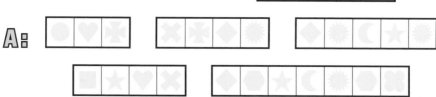

202

# WHICH IS WHICH?

There are plenty of pairs that people get confused, like vertical and horizontal or nearsighted and farsighted. In each pair, see if you know which one is which.

 MONKEY
APE

 PORTRAIT
LANDSCAPE

 STALACTITE
STALAGMITE

 TORNADO
HURRICANE

 PUPIL
IRIS

 LATITUDE
LONGITUDE

 TRICERATOPS
STEGOSAURUS

 REPUBLICAN
DEMOCRAT

 HOUR HAND
MINUTE HAND

NUT
BOLT

# WHITE HOUSE TOUR

Each of these sets of connected letters can be used the spell the full name of a US president. Start at the highlighted letter and proceed from letter to letter along the lines that connect them. You will need to return to some letters to spell each president's name.

**1**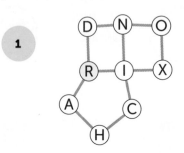

_____

**2**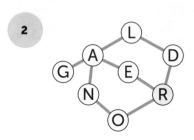

_____

**3**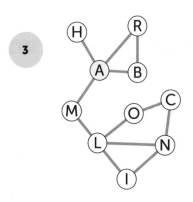

_____

**4**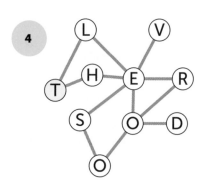

_____

**5**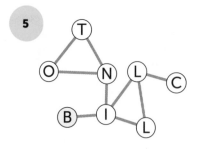

_____

**6**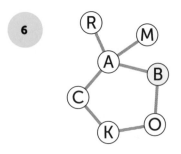

_____

# WILD WEST

Okay, buckaroos! Hidden in this here grid are things that're associated with the Wild West. When you've rounded 'em all up, payin' no mind to any punctuation or spaces between words, read the leftover letters (from left to right, top to bottom) to git yerself a Fascinatin' Fact about the Pony Express.

```
Y  O  B  W  O  C  C  P  H  I  T  T  O  N  S
N  L  Y  H  K  A  A  L  C  R  E  I  N  S  E
I  L  A  D  C  L  W  N  N  X  S  S  E  T  L
A  T  U  T  O  A  M  R  A  I  L  R  O  A  D
R  S  U  M  R  E  O  S  R  M  P  D  U  M  D
T  S  I  B  R  O  N  C  O  X  W  E  J  P  A
N  N  E  R  A  T  T  L  E  S  N  A  K  E  S
O  S  S  A  L  I  A  Y  G  G  I  H  L  D  T
G  E  R  T  A  H  N  O  L  L  A  G  N  E  T
A  E  O  N  M  O  A  C  O  Y  O  T  E  O  N
W  T  H  A  P  P  Y  T  R  A  I  L  S  H  S
```

| | | | |
|---|---|---|---|
| BRAWL | HORSE | PONY EXPRESS | STAGECOACH |
| BRONCO | JAIL | RAILROAD | STAMPEDE |
| CACTUS | LASSO | RANCH | TEN-GALLON HAT |
| COWBOY | LAWMAN | RATTLESNAKE | TEXAS |
| COYOTE | MONTANA | REINS | WAGON TRAIN |
| DUST | O.K. CORRAL | SADDLE | |
| HAPPY TRAILS | PALOMINO | SPURS | |

## FASCINATIN' FACT:

\_\_ \_\_\_\_ \_\_\_\_\_ _____

_____ _____.

# WINDOW DRESSING

First, name the six pictures and figure out where to put the words in the crossword. Then transfer the letters from the crossword to the numbered boxes at the bottom to get the answer to the riddle. Hint: Start by filling in the only four-letter word.

**Q** **What sign did the owner of the Halloween shop put in her front window?**

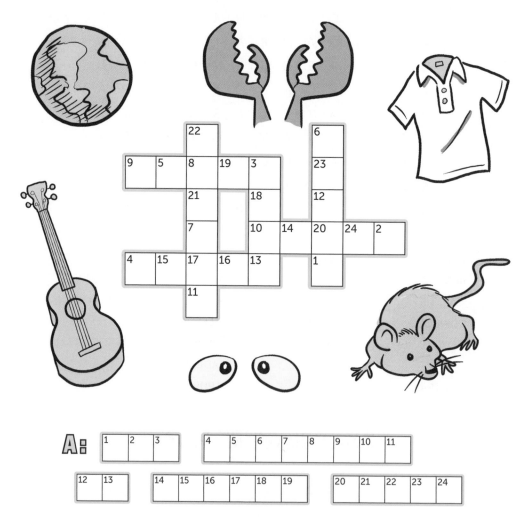

206

# WORD ORIGINS

## STRANGE ETYMOLOGIES

**W**hat does a butterfly have to do with butter? Why is a good-looking man said to be *handsome*? Why isn't a hammer called a nailer, or at least a banger?

*Etymology* is the study of word origins (not to be confused with *entomology*, the study of insects). Etymologists find out the history of the words we speak. After all, every word had to come from someplace.

Could *nice* mean anything other than, well, "nice"? Actually, yes—its original meaning, it turns out, is not so nice. The word began as the Latin word *nescius*, meaning "ignorant" or "stupid." Later the French started using it to mean "simpleminded." Over the centuries its meaning continued to shift, till it meant "delicate" or "tasteful." (We still use this meaning when we say somebody did a "nice" job). Believe it or not, *nice* has only meant "kind and pleasant" for about the last 150 years.

The meanings of words continue to change today. In the past few decades, the word *geek* has gone from meaning a very strange person (actually, a revolting type of circus performer) to someone who is very smart or who loves a particular subject. Similarly, the word *awful* used to mean "inspiring awe," like a majestic sight. But today, if you climbed Mount Everest and said the view was "awful," your Sherpa might be very annoyed!

Many words carry bits of history with them. The word *window* originates from an Old Norse word, *vindauga*. The first windows did not have glass panes; they were simply holes in a roof or wall. Naturally, these holes let in the breeze while allowing people to look out. The two concepts, wind (*vind*) and eye (*auga*), eventually evolved to *window*.

As for the origin of *handsome*, it wasn't originally used to describe people. It first meant "easy to handle," then "large" (as in a handsome amount of money), then "well-crafted," before it came to mean "good-looking."

As for *butterfly*, nobody is quite sure where it got its pretty name. Not even entomologists.

---

People used to say "God be with you" when leaving one another. What common word did this phrase turn into?

*For words made up by specific people (instead of evolving over time), see Neologisms: What's The Latest Word? For a quiz about the origin of some familiar phrases, see Say What?*

 THE PUZZLE

Fill in the blanks in each sentence with two words that sound the same. The first will end in X (like "lax") while the other one will end in K-S (like "lacks").

**1** We paid just 99 cents, plus _____ , for that little box of _____ we bought for the corkboard.

**2** In the time travel movie I just saw, a fierce Tyrannosaurus _____ arrives in the present and _____ everything it encounters, leaving a trail of destruction.

**3** The groom's _____ looks nice, but it'll look better after he _____ his shirt in.

**4** The bodybuilder continued to _____ his muscles until we could see little _____ of sweat on his forehead.

**5** After the jazz musician played her _____ on television, she received _____ full of fan mail.

**6** A beautiful, dangerous _____ escaped the big cat preserve after rust destroyed one of the _____ in the chain that held the gates closed.

**7** What started out as a figure molded out of soft _____ became an impressive iron statue once the artist broke open the cast with a few _____ of her mallet.

**8** That dumb thief thinks he can get into Fort _____ , where most of the country's gold is kept, if he just goes there and _____ on the door!

# X GAMERS

These kids want to compete in the X Games after seeing the cool equipment available. Read the clues and use logic to match each kid to the equipment he or she will use. There is only one way to match each kid with a different piece of equipment.

**RABIA** wants something that doesn't use a motor.
**STEPHEN** lives in a climate where it never snows, so winter sports are out.
**TERRENCE** prefers something with a seat.
**UMA** is the only one here with a license to drive a car.
**VERNON** wants something with racing stripes.
**WEN** wants to snowboard.

RABIA    STEPHEN    TERRENCE    UMA    VERNON    WEN

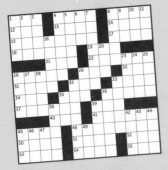

# PUZZLE BREAKERS

# XI FACTS ABOUT XWORD* PUZZLES

 **FUN FROM THE START**

The first crossword puzzle appeared in a newspaper in 1913 and was called a Word-Cross. (The name accidentally appeared as "Cross-Word" a few weeks later and eventually became "crossword.") The very first answer word across the top of the puzzle was FUN. There was no clue given—it was already filled in to show solvers how the puzzle worked.

 **WHATCHAMACALLIT?**

People who are really into solving or making crossword puzzles call themselves *cruciverbalists*.

 **ANY WAY YOU LOOK AT IT**

If you turn a newspaper crossword puzzle upside down, the way the black squares are arranged on the page will look the same. (Crossword constructors call this "rotational symmetry.")

 **READY . . . SET . . . SOLVE!**

There are crossword-solving competitions every year. Top solvers can complete some crossword puzzles in just two or three minutes, which is not much longer than it would take most people to write all the letters in the boxes if they were given the answers.

 **IN GOOD COMPANY**

In 1924, a woman asked her nephew, Dick Simon, where she could buy a book of crossword puzzles. He said there weren't any . . . then realized what a good idea this was. He and his friend Max Schuster pooled all their money and published the first crossword collection. The book was an immediate success, and not just because it came with a sharpened pencil! Today, the company they founded, Simon & Schuster, is one of the largest and most respected publishing companies in the world.

 **COMMON GROUND**

Most crossword puzzles for grownups have a theme so that the longest answers all have something in common or go together in some way. Part of the fun of solving the crossword is to discover this theme, which is often funny.

 **CONSTRUCTION WORK**

Crossword constructors have three jobs: making up the surprise theme of the puzzle, building a grid (with all the interlocking words), and writing the clues. If a puzzle is hard, it's usually because the clues are tricky, not because the words are unusual.

 This means "crossword."

 ## ONE FOR THE AGES

In 2013, the *New York Times* published a crossword that was cowritten by a 16-year-old boy and a 99-year-old woman. The answer AGE DIFFERENCE went across the middle of the puzzle, and the theme indicated by that answer was that words were made "different" by adding or subtracting the word "age" (like changing INSTANT MESSAGE to INSTANT MESS).

 ## FIRST THINGS FIRST

The question professional crossword constructors are asked most often is "Which do you write first, the words in the grid, or the clues?" The answer? They write the words in the grid first—it wouldn't make sense to write clues before answers are chosen.

 ## GET WITH THE PROGRAM

Can computers create crosswords? Usually it takes a person to come up with a theme and write clues. Many top crossword constructors do use special computer programs to help them find words to put in the grid, though computers are rarely used to decide all the words.

 ## ACROSS AND DOWN THE AISLE

More than once, a newspaper crossword has been used as a surprise marriage proposal. In each case, the solver (usually someone who solves the puzzle every day) gradually noticed their own name, their boyfriend's or girlfriend's name, and the phrase WILL YOU MARRY ME in the answers. This is all arranged in advance with the help of a professional crossword constructor.

In 1938, Alfred Butts invented a crossword-style board game he called Criss Cross Words. The name was changed ten years later to the name that's still used today for this popular game. Do you know what it is?

*For some unusual kinds of crossword puzzles, see One, Two, Three; Pinwheel; and Roundup. For an amazing story about crosswords during World War II, see Key Words.*

# X MARKS THE SPOT

In each maze, the object is to find one continuous path from START to the final . Your path must go through every box except the ones containing a skull and crossbones. You may only go through each box once, and your path may not cross itself. Diagonal moves are not allowed. The mazes get harder as you progress, and there is only one way to solve each one.

# X-RAY VISIONS

Only one of these X-ray images has the same details as the original picture in the middle. Can you tell which and spot the differences in the others?

# Y: THE PUZZLE

At the Y factory, special Y-shaped machines take two objects, add a letter Y, and mix up the results to create something new. In the first machine, for example, SAND and a CRAB are inserted. After adding a Y and scrambling all the letters, the machine creates CANDY BARS, which are shown on the conveyor belt below. Can you identify all the pairs of items in the remaining machines, and match each with the resulting object? The names of the final objects may be one or two words.

# YAKKITY YAK

Each list of words here will seem much more familiar if you say them out loud. That's because the words will sound like something you've heard before. For example, the first list, "say, burr, two, with, tyke, her," sounds like "saber-toothed tiger." If you get stuck, try having somebody say the words to you. The theme of the last list is for you to discover.

## PREHISTORIC ANIMALS

say, burr, two, with, tyke,          <u>saber-toothed tiger</u>

tries, air, it, hops                 _____

tire, henna, source, wrecks         _____

woo, limb, ham, myth                _____

fell, law, sir, wrap, tour          _____

stay, gas, Horace                   _____

terror, tack, till                  _____

## SCIENTISTS AND INVENTORS

toe, ma, said, hiss, Hun            _____

owl, bear, tie-ins, dine            _____

chain, goo, tall                    _____

bench, hum, an, fur, ankle, inn     _____

icy, canoe, tin                     _____

myrrh, reek, your, he               _____

jaw, urge, watching, dunk, are, four _____

## MYSTERY LIST

laboratory, tree, fir               _____

chair, munch, shipboard             _____

pass, it, downed                    _____

board, ark, holly                   _____

caw, curse, pan, yell               _____

sigh, beer, yen, huh, ski           _____

fur, wrench, Pooh, dull             _____

# YARD WORK

Can you get from YARD to SALE by changing just one letter in each word along the way? Here's a hint: Each word is one of the items offered on this front lawn. Start by looking for an item that's one letter different from YARD. If you get stuck, try solving from the bottom up. And don't forget to bargain!

**YARD**

**SALE**

# YEAR IN, YEAR OUT

The answer to each of these clues is a word or phrase that contains an abbreviation for a month of the year. Each abbreviation has already been placed, but the clues below are in random order. Can you get each clue and write it in the correct spot?

J A N ___ ___ ___ ___

___ ___ F E B ___ ___ ___

___ ___ ___ ___ ___ ___   ___ ___ ___ M A R ___ ___ ___

A P R ___ ___

M A Y ___ ___

J U N ___ ___ ___   ___ ___ ___

___ ___ ___ ___ ___   ___ ___ ___ J U L ___ ___ ___

___ A U G ___ ___ ___ ___

___ ___ ___ ___ ___ S E   P ___ ___ ___ ___

___ O C T ___ ___ ___ ___

___ ___ N O V ___ ___ ___ ___ ___ ___

___ ___ ___ ___ ___ D E C ___ ___

## CLUES

| | | |
|---|---|---|
| • Beatles song about an underwater vehicle that begins "In the town where I was born . . ." | • Mom and Dad's female child | • Phrase shouted if someone falls out of a boat |
| • Brushing and flossing prevent this | • Passengers would climb into this if their ship was sinking | • Playground item that kids climb around on |
| • Celebration planned in secret | • Person elected to be in charge of a town or city | • Romantic play written by William Shakespeare |
| • Item worn in the kitchen to keep your clothes clean | • Person who cleans the floors and walls at a school | • Word that describes animals that are awake at night |

# YO HO HO

To answer the riddle, look at the eight individual pieces at the bottom and find them in the large picture. When you find a piece, write the letters showing where it came from—the row first (gray skulls) and then the column (yellow skulls). When you've found them all, those letters will spell out, in order, the answer to the riddle. The location of the first piece has been filled in for you.

**Q** What happens to pirates who sing instead of steering the ship?

**A** They get _____.

# YOU MUST REMEMBER THIS

## MNEMONIC DEVICES

Can you recite the names of the eight planets, in order from the sun? If you can, you may have used a mnemonic to help. A *mnemonic* (or a "mnemonic device") is a trick for helping people remember something. The order of planets in our solar system, for example, is often linked to the phrase **M**y **V**ery **E**legant **M**other **J**ust **S**erved **U**s **N**achos. Each word in this sentence begins with a letter that is the first letter of each planet, in order: **M**ercury, **V**enus, **E**arth, **M**ars, **J**upiter, **S**aturn, **U**ranus, **N**eptune.

Can you name the five Great Lakes? They are Huron, Ontario, Michigan, Erie, and Superior, commonly remembered by the acronym HOMES. (An *acronym* is a word made from the first letters of other words.) To remember those same five lakes in order from west to east, try Super Man Helps Every One.

A good mnemonic is catchy enough to stick in your brain so it can be used as a tool to unlock the information it's based on. People have invented mnemonic devices to remember all sorts of things. Do you get mixed up between *stalagmites* (which grow from the cave floor) and *stalactites* (which grow down from the cave ceiling)? Some people remember that "mites" crawl on the floor, while tights ("tites") hang from a clothesline. Or that one word has a G (for "Ground") and the other has a C (for "Ceiling").

If you've ever played guitar, you've needed to remember the order of the strings in standard tuning. Instead of remembering the letters E-A-D-G-B-E, you might have preferred to remember Easter Angels Don't Give Broken Eggs, or Even Average Dogs Get Better Eventually, or this winner: Eddie Ate Dynamite—Good-Bye, Eddie!

Mnemonics can even be used to remember how to spell tricky words. If you sometimes write *hear* when you mean *here*, remember that we *hear* with our *ear*. How about remembering the difference between *principle* (a rule) and *principal* (a person)? Just remember the principal is your *pal*. To remember how to spell *rhythm*, pretend that it stands for Rhythm Helps Your Two Hips Move.

Of course, there's no guarantee you'll remember these mnemonics when you need them!

> "It's a priveledge to have two eyes and a leg." That's a mnemonic device that tells you how to spell the word "priveledge," which is spelled wrong here. What's the correct spelling, and how does the mnemonic help?

# YUCK!

To solve the riddle, use the clues to get as many of the answer words as you can. The clues are separated into ACROSS and DOWN, *but they are in random order*. (Two letters have been given as a starting hint.) When you've filled in all the words, use the symbols to transfer the right letters to the boxes at the bottom to spell the riddle's answer.

**Q:** **What's the grossest way to hurt your finger?**

**ACROSS**

"_____ mention it!"

An insect has six of these

One of the Great Lakes

Person who throws a party

**DOWN**

Black-and-white brand of cookies

Kept securely in the hand

Something a student studies for

STOP, YIELD, or NO U-TURN

**A:**

# **Z**: THE PUZZLE

The things listed here will fit into these boxes so that the words all interlock like a crossword puzzle. All the words include a double Z. By using the lengths of the words and the places where they cross as a guide, can you put them all in the correct spots? Hint: Start by placing the only five-letter word.

| | | |
|---|---|---|
| BEDAZZLE | GIZZARD | PAPARAZZI |
| BLIZZARD | GRIZZLY BEAR | PIZZA |
| BUZZARD | GUZZLE | PIZZAZZ |
| DAZZLING | JACUZZI | RAZZMATAZZ |
| DIZZIER | MIZZENMASTS | TWIZZLERS |
| DRIZZLE | MOZZARELLA | |

# ZANY BRAINIES

Each of these scenes can be described with a two-word phrase in which the two words rhyme with each other. For example, a drawing of a sign stuck on a structure with horses would be "stable label." Can you figure out the names of all eight?

1 ___ ___ ___ ___ ___ ___
___ ___ ___ ___ ___

2 ___ ___ ___ ___ ___ ___
___ ___ ___ ___ ___

3 ___ ___ ___ ___ ___
___ ___ ___ ___ ___

4 ___ ___ ___ ___ ___ ___ ___
___ ___ ___ ___ ___ ___

5 ___ ___ ___ ___ ___ ___
___ ___ ___ ___ ___ ___

6 ___ ___ ___ ___ ___ ___ ___
___ ___ ___ ___ ___ ___

7 ___ ___ ___ ___ ___
___ ___ ___ ___ ___

8 ___ ___ ___ ___ ___ ___ ___
___ ___ ___ ___ ___ ___ ___

# ZEUS RETURNS TO SUEZ

## A LOOK BACK AT REVERSALS

**R**eversals are like a cross between anagrams (see Anagrams: Why a Dormitory Is a Dirty Room) and palindromes (see Here's the Poop on Palindromes)—letters that spell one thing forward and something else backward. STOP, for example, becomes POTS. LIVED becomes DEVIL. If you put a BUS in reverse, it's a SUB. And REWARD becomes DRAWER.

Reversals might also be names. NEMO backward is OMEN. And OPRAH is HARPO—which Oprah Winfrey uses in the name of her company, Harpo Productions.

There are far fewer reversals than there are anagrams. This isn't too surprising, because in an anagram the letters can be rearranged into any order that works, but in a reversal there is only one rearrangement: backward.

However, there are some surprising examples of words that show up backward *inside* a longer word. You'll find an IGLOO in SCHOOLGIRL, NINTH in LIGHTNING, and MINOR in GERONIMO. The Beatles album REVOLVER contains the word LOVE in reverse—which was also the name of a later Beatles album.

You may find one reversal on your home bookshelf, if you have any books by Theo. LeSieg (two favorites are *Wacky Wednesday* and *Ten Apples Up on Top!*). If you read the author's last name backward, it spells Geisel—that's the real last name of Theodor Geisel, better known as Dr. Seuss.

In the 1970s, the company Evian began selling bottled water in the United States, which was uncommon at the time. People who objected to the idea of paying for water liked to point out that Evian spelled backward is *naive*, which means "easily fooled."

If you're ever stressed, think about the tasty options that are revealed when you read one of the words in this sentence backward. Which word?

*For a puzzle with words in reverse, see Return Trips.*

# ZIGS AND ZAGS

Each zigzag can be filled with a short word and a long word. First, identify each picture next to a zigzag and fill in the yellow diamonds. Then find a picture in the choices at the bottom whose name can be filled into the whole zigzag, using both the yellow and white diamonds and reading down and up in zigzag fashion, from left to right. The first one is filled in to show you how it works.

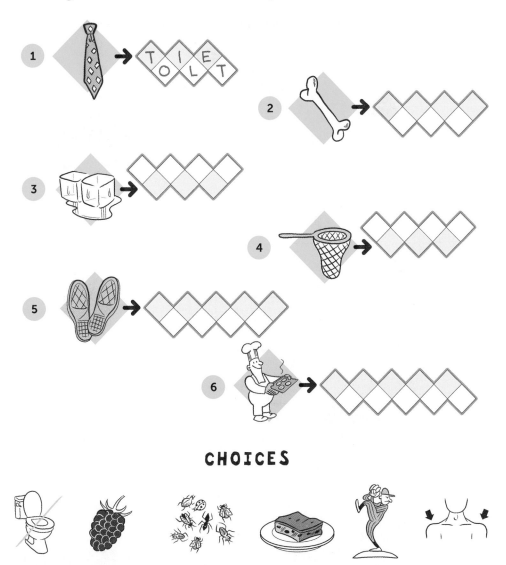

## CHOICES

# ZIP LINE

First, name the nine pictures and figure out where to put the words in the crossword. Second, transfer the letters from the crossword to the numbered boxes at the bottom to get the answer to the riddle. Careful—this one's tricky! Hint: Start by filling in the only six-letter word.

**Q** **Why did the driver speed past the movie theater?**

**A**

| 1 | 2 | | 3 | 4 | 5 | 6 | 7 | | 8 | 9 | 10 | 11 | | 12 | 13 | 14 | 15 |

| 16 | 17 | 18 | 19 | 20 | 21 | | 22 | 23 | 24 | | 25 | 26 | 27 | 28 | 29 | 30 | 31 |

# ZOM-BEES

Zom-bees don't make the usual straight beelines. Instead, they land on a flower, find a good starting point, and stumble from letter to letter in a winding path, like a maze. They only move to a space that touches the space they're on. Using this method, they can spell the names of three flowers in each of these honeycombs, using each letter once in an unbroken path. Can you find all the zom-bees' flowery trios?

# ZOODOKU

Each of the six animals shown is like a different number in a 6 × 6 sudoku puzzle.
Fill in each square with a different animal so that each animal appears once in
every row, column, and 3 × 2 shaded area.

# Z YOU LATER

A lengthy snake has camouflaged himself somewhere along this maze's path. When you've found the correct route from tail to head, darken your entire answer path (filling the space from edge to edge). Then hold the page up to a mirror and rotate it to reveal an appropriate message.

# THE ANSWERS

## A: THE PUZZLE

**BONUS MESSAGE:** An atlas has Japan, Canada, Alaska, Arkansas, Manhattan, and Atlanta.

## ADDITION EDITION

1. DESERT DESSERT
2. BRIDE BRIDGE
3. PLANT PLANET
4. GARAGE GARBAGE
5. CROW CROWN
6. STATE STATUE

## AHA!

**A:** OFF THE TOP OF HIS HEAD

## ALL THOSE OPPOSED

**GROUP 1:** dry, out, easy, ugly, day, guilty, empty. "Out" is the only word that doesn't end with the letter Y.

**GROUP 2:** poor, your, floor, for, war, odd, more. "Odd" is the only word that doesn't rhyme with "or."

**GROUP 3:** never, deep, present, man, sweet, better, remember. "Man" is the only word that contains a vowel other than E.

**A:** ODD MAN OUT

## ALPHA-CROSS

## AMPERSANDWICHES

1. HIDE & SEEK
2. PINS & NEEDLES
3. SHOW & TELL
4. SUGAR & SPICE
5. LOUD & CLEAR
6. THUNDER & LIGHTNING
7. MACARONI & CHEESE

## ANAGRAMS:

**WHY A DORMITORY IS A DIRTY ROOM**

TWELVE + ONE = ELEVEN + TWO

## ANIMAZING

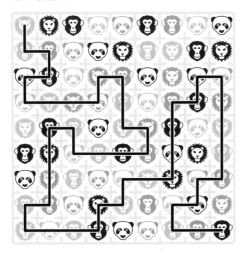

## ART BROKEN

**A:** IT'S POINTLESS

The differences in the bottom picture, from left to right, are: rear heel is taller; woman's right hand doesn't have bracelet; beret is different shade; face in picture on floor is smiling; chair rung is missing; hair of model is flipped down; drape passes in front of easel leg; top of easel is shorter; belt added.

## ASTRO-LOGICAL

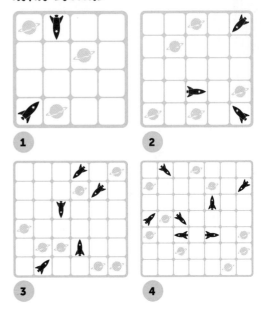

## AUTO MOTIVE

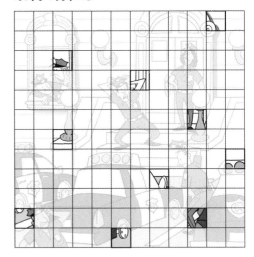

**A:** They had nothing to go on.

## B: THE PUZZLE

**ANSWER WORDS:** bride, tray, lasso, sides, witch, half, nametag
Words that cannot have BE at the beginning: bride, lasso, nametag

**A:** BE LO NG (belong/be long)

## BAKER'S DOESN'T

*TOP:* French bread is resting in light fixture; chain is missing from third light.

*LEFT WALL:* Sneaker is on bread rack; covered birthday cake has lit candles; layers in sliced cake don't line up; woman is decorating cake that has slice missing.

*REAR OF SHOP:* Picture of upside-down pineapple cake is upside down; baker is wearing baseball glove; bow on baker's apron has three strings; "3" on clock is in wrong position; feet are in rack of baked goods.

*REGISTER AREA:* Sign showing hours switches "thru" with "Thur"; doughnuts "special" gives 12 doughnuts for the price of 14; customer's feet are backward.

*DISPLAY COUNTER:* Cover on cookie tray is square at the top and round at the bottom; "free" samples cost money; cover on cake is shaped like a sliced cake; sign on glass repeats the word "on"; cup of hot coffee inside display case; girl is taking pie off shelf through glass; girl's father has three arms.

*RIGHT SIDE OF SHOP:* Black-and-white cookie parts don't line up; boy's pants have one short and one long leg; square on floor in front of boy is a hole; pattern on floor behind boy changes direction; man eating cake at table has liquid in spoon; chair facing man is missing front legs.

## BATTER UP!

**A:** UNLOCK THE CAR DOOR.

## BIG DRIPPER

### DIFFERENCES:

1.  Sprinkles missing from top
2.  Cherry rotated
3.  Layers in glass slant the other way
4.  (Match)
5.  Whipped cream lower in glass
6.  (Match)
7.  Top left hot fudge drip shorter
8.  Base column of glass longer

## BODY BUILDING

**BONUS MESSAGE:** Your arm or leg may fall asleep at school, but you may not.

## BOOK-TAC-TOE

**ROWS:** 1. Lightning shown 2. Bird in title
3. Both title words start with same letter.

**COLUMNS:** 1. Title has a word rhyming with "illy" 2. A kind of bow is shown 3. Title has a word that sounds like a letter (sea, you, tee)

**DIAGONALS:** 1. Arms up 2. "Sub" appears in title

## BRUNCH IS SERVED: PORTMANTEAU WORDS

a.  Labradoodle
b.  moped
c.  infomercial
d.  Popsicle
e.  intercom

## BUG OUT

1.  PAINT (ant)
2.  BLOCKBUSTER (locust)
3.  CHESS TOURNAMENT (hornet)
4.  BATTERIES NOT INCLUDED (beetle)
5.  FALSE ALARM (flea)
6.  WATERSPOUT (wasp)
7.  SMOOTHIE (moth)
8.  GYMNASTICS (gnat)
9.  ELECTRIC BLANKET (cricket)
10. BARBECUE (bee)

## C: THE PUZZLE

1. LOCK/CLOCK
2. LIPS/CLIPS
3. MATH/MATCH
4. PATH/PATCH
5. HAIR/CHAIR
6. UP/CUP

**Q:** Which note is easiest to sing if you're wearing glasses?

**A:** C SHARP (see sharp)

## CAP-TIVATING

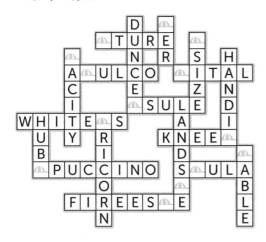

## CAST PARTY

The panels should be numbered as follows:
5, 3, 6, 2, 1, 4.

## CHICKEN AND EGG

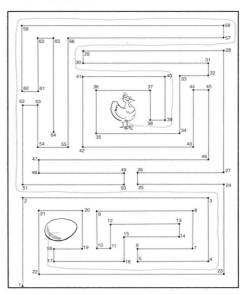

## CLOTHES CALL

**BONUS MESSAGE:** For a funny costume, wear any clothes and a sign saying: "Nudist on strike."

# CODE HARD FACTS:
## HOW TO SOLVE CRYPTOGRAMS

The decoded message is Hamlet's famous line "To be or not to be, that is the question."

## COLOR SCHEME

| S | T | A | R |
|---|---|---|---|
| T | R | U | E |
| A | U | R | A |
| R | E | A | D |

| N | O | P | E |
|---|---|---|---|
| O | K | A | Y |
| P | A | C | E |
| E | Y | E | S |

**A:** PUT ON A SECOND COAT

## CRAZY PHRAZIES

1. black belt in karate
2. brain wave
3. comic strips
4. disappearing ink
5. "Yellow Submarine"
6. quarterback
7. jack in the box
8. head over heels in love
9. right between the eyes
10. upside-down cake
11. listen up
12. man overboard

## CREEPY CRAWLIES

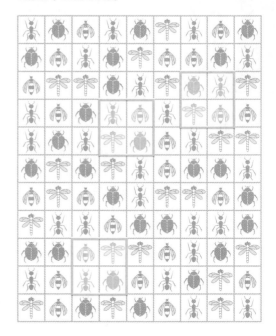

## D: THE PUZZLE

**CLUE:** IT HAS A BULL'S-EYE

**A:** DARTBOARD.

## DESERT CROSSINGS

## DICEDOKU

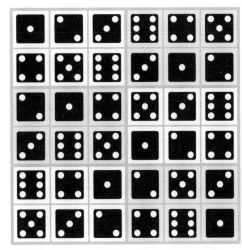

## DIDJA EVER SEE . . . ?

1. house fly
2. fish bowl
3. drum roll
4. brain wave
5. board walk
6. strawberry shake
7. vampire bat
8. curtain call
9. shoe box
10. waffle iron

## DINER TALK:
### SLINGING THE SLANG

**1**-d, **2**-c, **3**-b, **4**-e, **5**-a

## DIVIDE AND CONQUER

The sets are:

**THINGS WITH STRINGS** (tennis racket, bow and arrow, yo-yo, guitar)

**YELLOW THINGS** (smiley face, banana, school crossing sign, rubber duck)

**WORDS ENDING IN -OO** (kangaroo, igloo, bamboo, tattoo)

**THINGS THAT TURN** (faucet handle, revolving door, doorknob, ship's wheel)

## DOUBLE PLAY

```
H R E K C E D R I B B L E O A
J O I N T E D P E Y O K U E G
N J O N Y E D Y M M A H W D E
W J E O P A R D Y T D C E N N
H G T I H C I U E I S T H O T
A D O S H U B T B C N U L I E
M E M I T E B C A I K D M S N
M F N V D E L H O K B E D I A
Y D R A P O E J T U E R R V E
```

**BONUS MESSAGE:** Hope you enjoyed this double feature.

238

## DOUBLE SPACE

Changes that appear in picture on right (roughly from top to bottom): Rocket top is pointier; clipboard moves from one engineer on scaffolding to the other; diagonal on scaffolding changes direction; LIFT-OFF becomes BLAST-OFF; countdown time is 5:51:03 instead of 2:51:03; pipes below timer have moved up; capsule porthole is rectangular; moon becomes Earth in capsule monitor; dial near capsule monitor has changed to clock; panel of dials in capsule is unmirrored; bars on backpack are vertical; walking astronaut has no sideburn; hand on railing is bare; arm patch changes from flag to planet; circles on backpack are upside down; sleeve is missing one stripe; case in astronaut's hand has shifted knob; astronaut's other leg is forward; monitor showing rocket is widescreen; engineer's eyeglass frames are different; engineer's bow tie becomes necktie; fire extinguisher is smaller; engineer's coat is longer; UNITED STATES becomes UNTIED STATES; wire on floor has moved; head at bottom is bald; woman's long sleeve is gone; woman's headphones become headband.

they form the word UNDERGROUND. For another, this word overlaps with *itself*—its first three letters are the same as its last three:

## E: THE PUZZLE

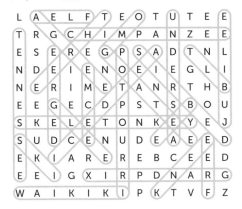

**BONUS MESSAGE:** Letters ending in the E sound are: B, C, D, E, G, P, T, V, Z.

## EARTHWORM

1. GROUND
2. ROUND TABLE
3. TABLET
4. TORCHES
5. ORCHESTRA
6. TRASH
7. SHALLOW
8. ALLOWANCE
9. ANCESTOR
10. STORE
11. EARTH
12. ARTHUR
13. URGENT
14. GENTLY
15. LYRIC
16. RICHER
17. HERMIT
18. MITTEN
19. TENTH
20. THUNDER
21. UNDER

Actually, the worm's last word has *two* connections to its first word. For one, together

## ENDLESS POSSIBILITIES

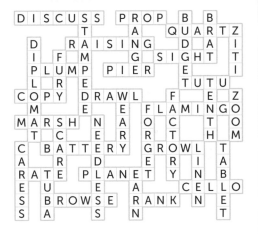

## ET CETERA

| | |
|---|---|
| 1. horn, hornet | 6. blank, blanket |
| 2. plan, planet | 7. bull, bullet |
| 3. ball, ballet | 8. pick, picket |
| 4. skill, skillet | 9. rock, rocket |
| 5. wall, wallet | 10. cabin, cabinet |

## EXTREME WORDS:
### HOLDERS OF THE WORD RECORDS

The word is *typewriter*.

By the way, these are the numbers that you can spell using the letters in *interchange-ability*: three, eight, nine, ten, thirteen, thirty, thirty-nine, eighty, eighty-nine, ninety, and ninety-eight.

## EYE EXAM

Clockwise from bottom left, the words are: eyeglasses, eyeball, eye candy, eye chart, eye doctor, eye socket, eye roll, eyewitness, eyelid, eye patch, eye shadow.

## F: THE PUZZLE

**NAMES OF COUNTRIES:**

France

Finland

Fiji

**KINDS OF BIRDS:**

falcon

flamingo

finch

**SYNONYMS FOR "PHONY":**

false

fictitious

fake

**FORMS OF TRANSPORTATION:**

ferry

fire engine

freighter

240

## FACE VALUE

| P | E | A | S | A | N | T |
|---|---|---|---|---|---|---|
| K | I | T | C | H | E | N |
| B | E | N | E | F | I | T |
| F | U | R | N | A | C | E |
| C | O | T | T | A | G | E |
| O | F | F | E | R | E | D |
| S | H | E | R | B | E | T |

A: Because it's the SCENTER.

## FAULT LINES

1. SELL ⟶ SMELL (M) (Added)
2. SPRING ⟶ STRING (T) (Replacement)
3. WAITER ⟶ WATER (I) (Deleted)
4. PRISON ⟶ POISON (O) (Replacement)
5. HUNTED ⟶ HAUNTED (A) (Added)
6. CURSED ⟶ CURED (S) (Deleted)
7. LIGHT ⟶ EIGHT (E) (Replacement)
8. LIES ⟶ LINES (N) (Added)
9. FINGERPAINTS ⟶ FINGERPRINTS (R) (Replacement)
10. THREAT ⟶ TREAT (H) (Deleted)
11. CLOWN ⟶ CROWN (R) (Replacement)
12. SALUTED ⟶ SALTED (U) (Deleted)
13. PATENTS ⟶ PARENTS (R) (Replacement)

A: TO ERRR IS HUMAN.

## FENCED IN

## FIGURE THAT

1. square dance
2. heartbreaking
3. Bermuda Triangle
4. fair and square
5. Arctic Circle
6. Oval Office
7. baseball diamond
8. Lone Star State
9. Times Square
10. "Circle of Life"

## FIT FOR A KING

**THE KINGS SHOULD BE NUMBERED AS FOLLOWS:**

| 3 | 6 | 9 |
|----|----|---|
| 10 | 8 | 2 |
| 4 | 11 | 5 |
| 12 | 1 | 7 |

## FOR YOUR EYES ONLY: HIDDEN MESSAGES

By reading the first letter of each paragraph, you can reveal the hidden message HIDE AND SEEK.

## FRANKENWORDS

| | |
|---|---|
| COBWEB | SHADOW |
| FRIGHT | TERROR |
| GOBLIN | ZOMBIE |

## FROG IN THE THROAT

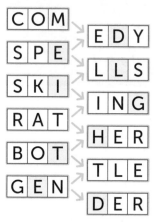

| | |
|---|---|
| C O M | → E D Y |
| S P E | → L L S |
| S K I | → I N G |
| R A T | → H E R |
| B O T | → T L E |
| G E N | → D E R |

**A:** DELIGHTED (de-lighted)

## FROM END TO END

## G: THE PUZZLE

1. bully, buggy
2. sorry, soggy
3. bottles, boggles
4. err, egg
5. mummy, muggy
6. jotted, jogged
7. muffle, Muggle
8. buzzed, bugged
9. ripping, rigging
10. trimmer, trigger

# "GATOR ATTACKS PUZZLE EXPERTS":
## AND OTHER STRANGE HEADLINES

1. A tree located a stolen painting. / A stolen painting was found near a tree.
2. A human eye has fallen off a shelf. / Eye drops have been removed from store shelves.
3. An escaped wallaby got in trouble for using a huge fishing net. / A huge fishing net was used in order to catch an escaped wallaby.
4. Two students shouted so loudly at each other that their teacher went deaf. / A court hearing involving a teacher ended when people began arguing loudly with each other.
5. The coast of Washington is slowly disappearing because tuna fish are nibbling it away. / The tuna are easy to catch near the coast of Washington.

6. Satellites have discovered alien whales approaching our planet. / Satellites looking down at Earth are able to locate and follow the paths of whales.

## GEM-DANDY

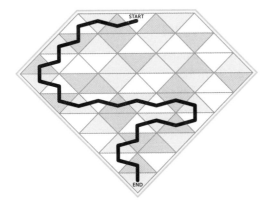

## GEO-LOGICAL

1. Havana. Theme: places with names that have only the vowel A
2. Madison, Wisconsin. Theme: cities named after US presidents
3. Liverpool. Theme: places whose names begin and end with the same letter
4. Pittsburgh, Pennsylvania. Theme: cities whose names begin with the same letter as the state they're in
5. Redmond, Washington. Theme: locations with a color in their names
6. Buenos Aires. Theme: places whose names have two words

## GOING GREEN

**BONUS MESSAGE:** In the future, children may ask "Why is the sky brown?"

## GOODNIGHT MOO

The words are: pie, tail, spear, statue, fireman, umbrella, drumstick, microscope

A: IT IS PASTURE BEDTIME (past your bedtime).

## GRADE EXPECTATIONS

The panels should be numbered as follows: 3, 2, 6, 5, 1, 4.

## GRAVEYARD SHIFT

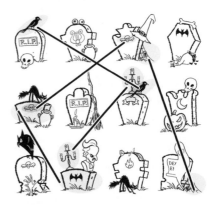

## GRIDLOCK

| | | | |
|---|---|---|---|
| A D D | T E A | G R O W | T R I P |
| T R Y | U R N | L A V A | H O S E |
| E Y E | B A T | O V E R | A B L E |
| | | W E N T | W E E K |

## GUESS LIST

**MONTHS**

```
            S
  N O V E M B E R
            P           M A Y
  M         T     F       P
  A   D E C E M B E R     R
  R         M     B       I
  O C T O B E R   U   J U L Y
  H         E     A
    J U N E R     R   A U G U S T
  J A N U A R Y   Y
            E
```

**SENSES**

```
  S I G H T
  M     E
  E   T A S T E
  L   R     O
  L   I     U
      N     C
      G     H
```

**CHESS PIECES**        **GREAT LAKES**

```
  R O O K           S         O
      N       H U R O N       N
      K I N G     P           T
      G           E           A
  B I S H O P     R           R
      T     A     M I C H I G A N
          P A W   O           O
        Q U E E N E R I E
```

# GUY GARGOYLE, GIRL GARGOYLE:
## TING TWUSTERS

Tongue twisters are known as "finger fumblers"
in American Sign Language.

## H: THE PUZZLE

1. ours (hours)
2. earth (heart)
3. height, then (eight, ten)
4. tree (three)
5. haunt (aunt)
6. ear (hear)
7. scrimp, spark, pleasant, steep (shrimp, shark, pheasant, sheep)
8. rice, forty (rich, forth)

A: HAIR CONDITIONER / AIR CONDITIONER

## HARDY HAR HAR

### DIFFERENCES:

1. Woman's hair is smaller.
2. Woman's skirt doesn't flare.
3. Can is shorter.
4. Man's arm is bent more.
5. Space near woman's finger is filled in.
6. Man's hair is shorter.
7. (Match)
8. Spring-loaded snake is closer to can.
9. Woman has tongue.
10. Man's ear is higher.

## HAVING IT BOTH WAYS

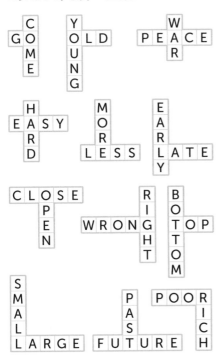

## HOLED-UP NOTE

## HERE'S THE POOP . . .
### ON PALINDROMES

The motto of the Three Musketeers is "All for one and one for all!"

## HIT OR MISS

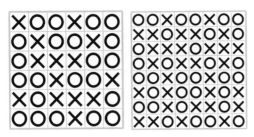

## HOT STUFF

**BONUS MESSAGE:** Lightning is fifty thousand degrees Fahrenheit or so, which is much hotter than the sun.

245

## I: THE PUZZLE

**OBJECTS:** emoji, pi, Hawaii, bikini, safari, Miami, graffiti, pepperoni, confetti, lei, origami, Leonardo da Vinci, broccoli, spaghetti, cacti, ski, rabbi, taxi, samurai, sushi.

## ICE PACK

## INCREDIBLE EDIBLES

1. taco tack
2. bacon baton
3. cake cage
4. burger burper
5. pear tear
6. gravy grave
7. waffle raffle
8. butter butler

## ISLAND TOUR

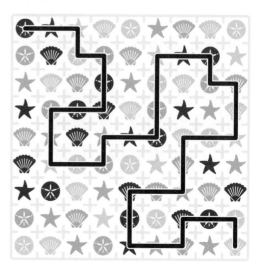

## IS THAT A FACT?

1. True. In order for Coca-Cola to patent the formula, they would have to share their secret recipe with the patent office, which they do not want to do.

2. Excellent. Einstein was a brilliantly gifted student in both math and science, just as you'd expect. His grades in some of his other classes were not as great, which led to him failing an important entrance exam. That exam may be the source of the mistaken belief that Einstein was a bad student overall.

3. Fireproof. *Flammable* is a word, but *inflammable* and *flammable* actually mean the same thing: "easily set on fire."

4. Cloth. All US "paper" currency is made from a combination of 75 percent cotton and 25 percent linen.

5. Less than 20,000 leagues. In fact, the deepest the submarine goes is four leagues. (A league is about 3.5 miles.) The title refers to how *far* the submarine travels, not how *deep* it goes. If a submarine went 20,000 leagues below the ocean's surface, it would go through the Earth's core, come out the other side, and keep going through the distance of five more Earths!

6. Neither—the odds are the same no matter the numbers.

7. You'd get in trouble because an octopus has no bones.

8. True. It was not called World War I until the beginning of World War II, since nobody knew there would be a second one. President Wilson had died by then. During his lifetime, the war was called "The World War" or "The Great War."

9. Neither—they have the same number, seven. Each giraffe neck bone is about 10 inches long, about 10 times longer than a human neck bone.

10. Up and down. Hope you got this one right.

11. The dog. *Canariae* is Latin for "of dogs," which by at least one account used to roam the islands. The bird known as the canary was actually named after the islands.

12. The sound through the iron rod. Sound travels through gases most slowly (about 350 meters per second through air, as in that hollow tube), through liquids faster (about 1,500 meters per second through water), and through solids fastest (about 5,000 meters per second through iron, and 12,000 meters per second through diamond!).

# IT ALL ADDS UP:
## MAGIC SQUARES

| 16 | 3 | 2 | 13 |
|----|----|----|----|
| 5 | 10 | 11 | 8 |
| 9 | 6 | 7 | 12 |
| 4 | 15 | 14 | 1 |

## IT'S NO USE!

**THE MISSING ITEMS ARE:**

1. JACKET: zipper half
2. SCISSORS: screw or bolt connecting halves where they cross
3. TEAKETTLE: handle
4. BASEBALL MITT: webbing between thumb and first finger
5. LOCK: hole on top for closing and securing the lock
6. STOVE: oven handle
7. LIGHTBULB: threads at bottom to screw in
8. EASEL: rear leg

## J: THE PUZZLE

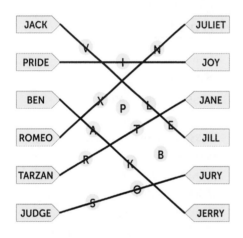

| | |
|---|---|
| JACK | JULIET |
| PRIDE | JOY |
| BEN | JANE |
| ROMEO | JILL |
| TARZAN | JURY |
| JUDGE | JERRY |

A: PB (PB&J)

## JAM SESSIONS

1. bananas, nasty, typo, pour, urgent, gentle, legal, gallon, long
2. taste, steal, also, soap, appear, pearl, least, Easter, error
3. surfing, finger, errand, random, omen, engrave, gravel
4. rushed, hedge, Gemini, minimum, mummy, myth, thank, ankle, leap

## JEWEL BOX

Take one jewel from the compartment in the left column, three rows down (where there are four jewels), and move it to the top row, into the compartment on the right (where there are three jewels).

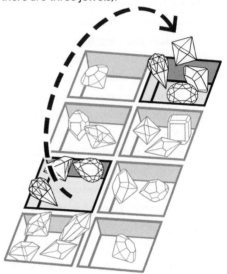

## JOB OPENINGS

1. PLUMBER
2. SCIENTIST
3. PAINTER
4. COMPOSER
5. ASTRONAUT
6. LUMBERJACK
7. TAILOR
8. ARCHITECT

## JUMPING THROUGH HOOPS:
### WRITING WITH RIDICULOUS RESTRICTIONS

*Green Eggs and Ham*

## K: THE PUZZLE

## KANGAGRAMS

1. BURST
2. MARKET
3. BLOSSOM
4. CHICKEN
5. FRAGILE
6. FEAST
7. CHOCOLATE
8. MYSELF
9. ENCOURAGE
10. DECEASED
11. EVACUATE
12. ASTOUND
13. MASCULINE

## KEEPING YOUR WORD

DATE, ADDRESS, STORY, SCHOOL, NOTE
The final word is BOOK.

## KEY WORDS:
### THE SECRET HISTORY OF CROSSWORDS IN WWII

b. During the war, the school's teachers and students had been evacuated from London and moved next to a military camp. One of the boys said the soldiers talked about their plans in front of him, and he suggested Dawe use the code words in his puzzles. He believed that hundreds of other students must have heard the words, too.

## KNIGHT WATCH

### DIFFERENCES:

1. Emblem on the back of the horse has a different top.
2. Horse's rear legs have changed position.
3. Collar ring is missing from helmet.
4. Feather points downward.
5. (Match)
6. Decorative cloth has more ruffles.
7. (Match)

## KNOTTY SITUATIONS

1.
| O | T | I |
|---|---|---|
| A | H | C |

5.
| R | E | G |
|---|---|---|
| O | N | A |

2.
| D | E | L |
|---|---|---|
| E | Y | A |

6.
| A | D | N |
|---|---|---|
| S | S | E |

3.
| A | M | A |
|---|---|---|
| B | A | L |

7.
| S | M | A |
|---|---|---|
| W | E | N |

4.
| S | K | A |
|---|---|---|
| R | E | T |

8.
| L | E | R |
|---|---|---|
| T | T | A |

**A:** They make ends meet.

## KOOKY CUTTERS

**AL** cuts Ehsan's hair.

**BRITTANY** cuts Fran's hair.

**CARL** cuts Al's hair.

**DAVE** cuts Brittany's hair.

**EHSAN** cuts Carl's hair.

**FRAN** cuts Dave's hair.

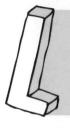

## L: THE PUZZLE

WINDMILLS
SEAGULL
BALLOON
FAREWELL
WILLIAM
VALLEY
LOLLIPOP
SYLLABLES
ALLOWANCE
WILLOW

**A:** To make his MEOW MELLOW.

## LAST WORD

1. BOOKKEEPER
2. DETECTED
3. CHEAT (HEAT, EAT, AT)
4. HERE (THERE)
5. MARS (MARK, MARY)
6. PRAISING (RAISIN)
7. STRAW (WARTS)
8. SHOUT and THORN (SOUTH and NORTH)

9. RUST (RSTU)

10. CROSSWORD (SWORD)

11. AREA (3 syllables) becomes ARE (1 syllable)

12. AMBIDEXTROUS

13. INTESTINES (If you cut this word in half, both halves will have the same letters.)

14. CRUDE (RUDE)

The last word remaining is almost last, because it's LEAST.

## LAW AND REORDER

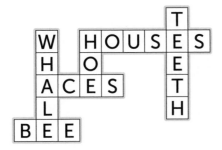

A: Because he stole the show.

## LIST BREAKERS

### THINGS AT A PICNIC

1. WATERMELON
2. CORN ON THE COB
3. TABLECLOTH
4. FRUIT SALAD
5. PAPER PLATES
6. FRIED CHICKEN
7. KETCHUP
8. HAMBURGER BUNS
9. POTATO CHIPS
10. NAPKINS

## HALLOWEEN COSTUMES

1. WITCH
2. FRANKENSTEIN
3. LUMBERJACK
4. NINJA
5. SKELETON
6. WIZARD
7. SUPERHERO
8. POLICE OFFICER
9. HEADLESS HORSEMAN
10. ZOMBIE

## LISTEN HERE

### US STATES

1. Pennsylvania
2. Illinois
3. Arizona
4. Connecticut
5. Rhode Island
6. Tennessee
7. Wisconsin

### COUNTRIES OF THE WORLD

1. Germany
2. Singapore
3. Switzerland
4. France
5. Egypt
6. Uruguay
7. Thailand

### US TOURIST ATTRACTIONS

1. Niagara Falls
2. Statue of Liberty
3. Lincoln Memorial
4. Grand Canyon
5. San Diego Zoo
6. Hoover Dam
7. Golden Gate Bridge

### BODIES OF WATER

1. Lake Superior
2. Panama Canal
3. Pacific Ocean
4. Mediterranean Sea
5. Gulf of Mexico
6. Mississippi River
7. Chesapeake Bay

## LOOK BOTH WAYS BEFORE CROSSING:
### WORD SQUARES

| C | R | A | B |
|---|---|---|---|
| R | A | C | E |
| A | C | T | S |
| B | E | S | T |

## LOOK OUT BELOW

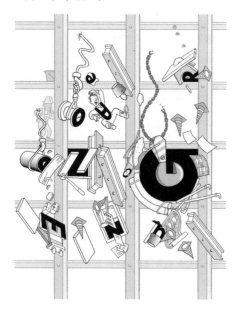

## LUMBER PARTY

The panels should be numbered as follows: 4, 3, 6, 1, 2, 5.

## M: THE PUZZLE

```
                    M I S S I S S I P P I
              M I S S O U R I
          M A R Y L A N D
      M I N N E S O T A
          M A S S A C H U S E T T S
              M A I N E
      M I C H I G A N
```

## MADE TO ORDER

**BREAKFAST FOODS:**

doughnuts, croissant, home fries

**MAIN COURSES:**

hamburger, crab cakes, spaghetti

**ICE CREAM FLAVORS:**

chocolate, pistachio, Rocky Road

## MATCH MAKING

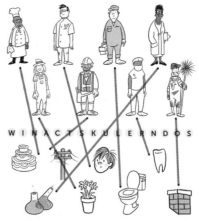

A: WICK ENDS (weekends)

# MAZES THAT GROW ON YOU:
## THE WINDING WORLD OF HEDGE MAZES

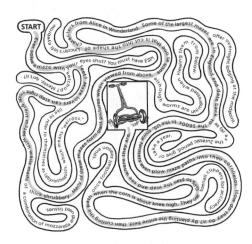

Ever solve a maze with your feet? Maze lovers can step right inside giant mazes with walls made of thick shrubbery. Many of these mazes form giant pictures when viewed from above, such as one that is cut into the shape of characters from Alice in Wonderland. Some of the largest mazes are in England and date back to the 1600s. In the US, some farmers even plow maze paths into their cornfields. How do they do it? By planting the entire field, then cutting the path when the corn is about knee high. They use GPS to plan the map and see where they are.

## MIND YOUR P'S AND Q'S

1. speak, squeak
2. part, quart
3. pick, quick
4. spare, square
5. pits, quits
6. paint, quaint
7. pack, quack

## MIXED MESSAGES

1. ACTORS and CO-STAR
2. MEASURED and MADE SURE
3. DECIMAL POINT and I'M A PENCIL DOT
4. ARCHAEOLOGIST and I GO SEARCH A LOT
5. RED TAG SALE and GREAT DEALS

## MONEY TALKS

1. Inventor Oiling Unicycle
2. Iguana Obeying Umpire
3. Igor Opening Umbrella
4. Insects Ordering Ukulele
5. Infant Observing Unicorns

## MOVIE CREW

### INTERESTING FACT:

Directors film movie scenes out of order.

## N: The Puzzle

1. RU(N)G
2. BAR(N)
3. BU(N)S
4. WI(N)DOW
5. S(N)AIL
6. WI(N)G

A: LOG (LO(N)G)

## NAMING NAMES

1. Molly Kewel (molecule)
2. Kent Seawell (can't see well)
3. Reed Enright (read and write)
4. Rhea Polster (reupholster)
5. Dan DeLyon (dandelion)
6. Doris Tuck (door is stuck)
7. Doug Boanes (dug bones)
8. Jim Shortz (gym shorts)
9. Lee King (leaking)
10. Barb Dwyer (barbed wire)
11. Carrie Oakey (karaoke)
12. Robin Banks (robbing banks)

## NATURE TRAIL

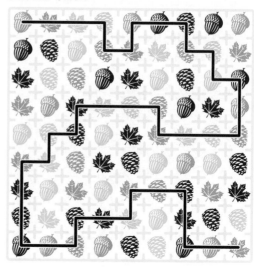

# NEOLOGISMS:
## WHAT'S THE LATEST WORD?

Googol. In 1920, mathematician Edward Kasner proposed this immense number and asked his young nephew Milton Sirotta what to call it. In 1997, Milton's word was misspelled "Google" when the company's founders were searching for a name that suggested large amounts of information.

## NO COACHING!

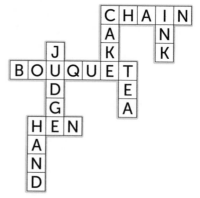

A: He had a king and queen but no jack.

## NOT EGGS-ACTLY

### DIFFERENCES:

1. Hen's far wing is lower.
2. Dragon is smaller.
3. Eggshell is face up.
4. (Match)
5. Nesting box has extra planks.
6. Chick on left has shifted.
7. Wattle (under beak) is not colored.
8. (Match)
9. Tail feathers are shorter.

## NOTE WORTHY

**BITA:** cello
**JUSTIN:** drums
**KATIE:** trombone
**MICHAEL:** saxophone
**TIM:** trombone
**VALERIE:** tambourine

## NOTHING BUT NET

## NOW HEAR THIS!

**INTERESTING FACT:** Ping-Pong is named for the sounds of the game.

## NUMBER CRUNCHING:
### THE BEALE CIPHERS

Don't count on it.

## 0: THE PUZZLE

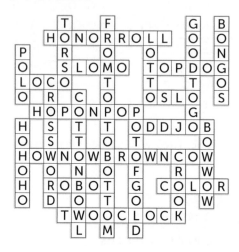

## OBSTACLE COURSE

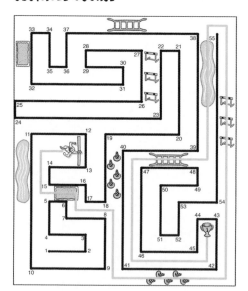

## O, I C!

E Y E O T E Y E E E S E A S Y
L U R O M K E C A H N E N M H
E E A P N E N I T H E E A E W
V X T E A F O R T W O L R L H
A Y C N D R Y Y O U N A L G O
T R E E S D N A T I A W U O Y
O E A M S L A N I G I R O V H
R L O Y K S A Y O R P Y N O W
U R O E N O M E N A A E S C K

NE1 (anyone)

DL (deal)

EZ (easy)

LF8R (elevator)

MT (empty)

NME (enemy)

NRG (energy)

NV (envy)

XS (excess)

LO (hello)

RHNL (original)

PNO (piano)

CNMNE (sea anemone)

CL (seal)

CI2I (see eye to eye)

T42 (tea for two)

YOY (why oh why?)

U8NC (you wait and see)

**BONUS MESSAGE:** UROK can mean either "you are okay" or "you rock."

## ONE, TWO, THREE

| | | | | | | | | | | | |
|---|---|---|---|---|---|---|---|---|---|---|---|
| COU | PO | N | | | FLA | SHE | S | | | | |
| S | T | OVE | | BOO | M | ER | ANG | | | | |
| IN | TER | L | OC | K | ING | | | | | | |
| | | S | TOP | | OS | TRI | CH | | | | |
| QUI | TE | | US | HER | | PLE | ASE | | | | |
| LL | A | MA | | CU | BA | | | | | | |
| | | RAT | T | LES | N | A | KE | | | | |
| FI | SH | H | OOK | | DI | AR | Y | | | | |
| G | ALL | ON | | | T | ON | S | | | | |

## ON THE HOUSE

| A | N | C | H | O | R |
|---|---|---|---|---|---|
| | | I | G | L | O | O |
| B | U | T | T | O | N |

| | | T | U | R | T | L | E |
|---|---|---|---|---|---|---|---|
| S | H | E | P | H | E | R | D |
| J | E | S | T | E | R |

| | | K | N | I | G | H | T |
|---|---|---|---|---|---|---|---|
| B | A | T | T | E | R | Y |
| | | I | S | L | A | N | D |
| | | L | A | D | D | E | R |

**A:** Hit the nail on the head.

## OPPOSITE DAY

| | | |
|---|---|---|
| YEN/SO | → | YES/NO |
| FIT/THAN | → | FAT/THIN |
| COAL/WORM | → | COOL/WARM |
| FLESH/STARE | → | FRESH/STALE |
| SAPPY/HAD | → | HAPPY/SAD |
| LOFT/SOUND | → | LOST/FOUND |
| WED/TRY | → | WET/DRY |
| SHARD/PULL | → | SHARP/DULL |
| DIVE/LIE | → | LIVE/DIE |
| FAN/REAR | → | FAR/NEAR |
| FEED/HEAT | → | FEET/HEAD |

## OUT ON A LIMB

1. swan (wa**s wan**dering)
2. ostrich (M**ost rich**)
3. flamingo (**flaming o**ut)
4. sparrow (cla**sp arrow**s)
5. pelican (cha**pel I can**oed)
6. hawk (wit**h awk**ward)
7. cardinal (post**card in al**most)
8. pheasant (catastro**phe as ant**icipated)
9. stork (ne**st or k**ept)

## OXYMORONS:
### JUMBO SHRIMP AND OTHER INSTANT CLASSICS

PAID VOLUNTEER

UNBELIEVABLY REALISTIC

GROWING SMALLER

FINAL DRAFT

STRANGELY FAMILIAR

SECOND BEST

COMPLETELY UNFINISHED

DEAFENING SILENCE

AWFULLY GOOD

## P: THE PUZZLE

The two Ts in TORTOISE can be changed to Ps to spell PORPOISE.

By the way, you can also change the two Ts in TURTLE to Ps, but you won't change its species—just its color.

## PAIR-OFFS

The words are: pit, couch, penny, dog, baby, rug, skis

**A:** THE DARK

## PANGRAMS: FROM A TO Z

The word is UNCOPYRIGHTABLE.

## PARTY-HOPPING

| E A R T H | E Y E S |
| B E A R | E G G S |
| R O O F | T E N T |
| E A G L E | A P P L E |
| C O V E R | S H O E |

**A:** They are often leap overs (sleepovers).

## PET PEEVE

1. J, Q, K, A
2. W
3. I, O
4. F, H (fire, hire)
5. U
6. B, C, D, G, P, T, V, Z
7. Y, N (yes, no)
8. S, M, L

**A:** REX ("Wrecks")

## PICTURED POSTCARDS

1. The Sphinx (Egypt)
2. The Leaning Tower of Pisa (Italy)
3. The Taj Mahal (India)
4. Stonehenge (England)
5. The Eiffel Tower (France)
6. The Great Wall of China (China)
7. The Sydney Opera House (Australia)
8. Easter Island (Chile)

## PINWHEEL

## PLAYING THE NUMBERS:

### SUDOKU

c. There are 362,880 different orders possible. (The way to get this number is to multiply $9 \times 8 \times 7 \times 6 \times 5 \times 4 \times 3 \times 2 \times 1$.) The number of possible $9 \times 9$ sudoku grids, however, is a bit larger. That number is 22 digits long.

## PLAY IT BY EAR

**DO:** doll, dollar, door, doughnuts

**RE:** record (on door), recycle (symbol), refrigerator, remote

**MI:** microphone, milk, mirror, mittens

**FA:** faces, fan, father, faucet

**SO:** soap, socks (on auditioning singer), socket, sofa (also song, being sung in the audition)

**LA:** laces, ladder, ladybug, lamp

**TI:** tiara, tie, tights, tissues

## POINT BLANK

1. POP-UP BOOK
2. DOWN JACKET
3. UPSIDE-DOWN CAKE
4. "WHAT'S UP, DOC?"
5. HAND-ME-DOWN
6. UP IN THE AIR
7. MELTDOWN
8. "BATTER UP!"
9. DRESS UP
10. DOWN UNDER
11. "NOTHING UP MY SLEEVE"
12. CRACKING UP
13. TOUCHDOWN
14. WHAT GOES UP MUST COME DOWN

## PRESTO CHOOSE-O

The last word you landed on was MAGIC.

## Q: THE PUZZLE

## QUACKING WISE

1. RAM + BONE + KEY − BAKER = MONEY
2. PIE + CANNON + MOUTH − MOON − INCH = PEANUT
3. BAG + TIRE − GATE + HOOD + CAST + WELL − TWO − SHOE = BIRDCALL
4. CAR + TIES − TEA + CAKE + TOP − SOAP = CRICKET
5. COW + RING − WIG = CORN

PEANUT
CRICKET
CORN
MONEY
BIRDCALL

**A:** Put it on my bill.

259

## QUAD-WRANGLES

1. BODY PARTS: foot, lips, knee, neck
2. MUSICAL INSTRUMENTS: tuba, oboe, drum, harp
3. INSECTS: moth, flea, wasp, gnat
4. WEATHER: snow, heat, wind, rain
5. ANIMAL SOUNDS: buzz, meow, oink, roar

## QUIET!

1. CORE: silent E
2. BERET: silent T
3. ISLAND: silent S
4. LINCOLN: silent L
5. COLUMN: silent N
6. FRIENDS: silent I

A: The SILENT man is the best to LISTEN to.

## QUO-TRIVIA

1. EEYORE
2. VENUS
3. ORANGE
4. NOON
5. SKIING
6. *PEANUTS*
7. BIOGRAPHY
8. PUTT
9. WASHINGTON
10. HELLO
11. THIRTY
12. TWINE

Mark Twain said: "There is nothing so annoying as to have two people talking when you're busy interrupting."

## Q: WHAT DO YOU CALL THE HISTORY OF THE RIDDLE?
### A: A BUNCH OF OLD JOKES

The riddle's answer is "today." Just before today arrived, it was called "tomorrow," and as soon as it's done, it will be called "yesterday." As the riddle says, "I change my name three days in a row"—meaning from "tomorrow" to "today" to "yesterday," over the course of three days—while being only one day long.

# R: THE PUZZLE

1. F(R)OG
2. PEA(R)S
3. TI(R)E
4. C(R)ANE

**Q:** What word costs more when you drop the letter R?

**A:** FREE (becomes FEE)

## RAIN CHECK

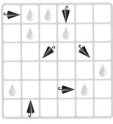

## RE-PAIR SHOP

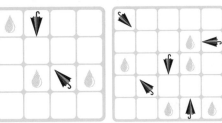

RIBBON ESCALATOR
SPATULA WAND
FLAG LASSO
BACON TRACTOR
SPAGHETTI EYE
LEG GRAPEFRUIT
MUSTACHE ARTIST

**A:** The highlighted words are all things that you might BREAK.

## RETURN TRIPS

1. gum, mug
2. keep, peek
3. gulp, plug
4. pins, snip
5. devil, lived
6. knits, stink
7. parts, strap
8. repaid, diaper
9. drawer, reward
10. stressed, desserts

## REVOLUTIONARY IDEA

The words are: kit, wave, shark, turkey, unicorn, flagpole, slingshot

**A:** It was a turning point.

## RHYME SPREE

quill, bill/beak, leak/drip, rip/tear, hair/part, heart/love, glove/mitt, pit/hole, goal/net, jet/plane, pain/ache, steak/meat, feet/toes, nose/snout, trout/fish, dish/plate, crate/box, rocks/stones, bones/skeleton, gelatin

# RHYMING SLANG:
## THAT'S USING YOUR LOAF!

"Tart" rhymes with "fart"!

## RIPPLE PLAY

```
E E C L L E W G N I H S I W U T
D C S N P B U C K E T Q I U M E
I B P O R A I N C L O U D S E A
R R O O H T L A N A C I S A A P
E L N G R H E A Q U A R I U M O
M N G A I T N E K T S T E Y C T
U O E L P U D D L E I G S E X I X
L P A E R B C E N T N U A W K A
F T H T O O B G N I K N U D E R
```

**INTERESTING FACT:** Cucumbers are ninety-six percent water.

## ROCKET RACKET

1. rocket, racket
2. dawn, down
3. decade, decide
4. sample, simple
5. computing, competing
6. red, rid
7. thank, think
8. better, bitter
9. genius, genies
10. while, whole
11. some, same
12. must, most
13. lump, lamp
14. fist, fast
15. messed, missed
16. linger, longer
17. wandering, wondering
18. step, stop
19. none, nine

## ROUNDUP

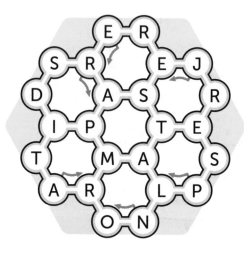

**A:** A STAMP

## RUSH HOUR

The panels should be numbered as follows: 4, 6, 3, 1, 5, 2.

## S: The Puzzle

1. CRAWLS
2. STRAIN
3. NAILS
4. SWORD
5. SPLATTER
6. WINGS
7. SCRAWL
8. SNAIL
9. PLATTERS
10. STRUCK
11. WORDS
12. SCAR
13. SWING

The leftover words are STRAIN, STRUCK, and SCAR. Moving their Ss to the end gives you three kinds of vehicles: TRAINS, TRUCKS, and CARS.

## SAND-WHICH

CASTLE

TRAP

DUNE

DOLLAR

BAGS

STORM

PAPER

CRAB

BOX

## SAY WHAT?

### THE STRANGE ORIGINS OF FAMILIAR PHRASES

| | | | |
|---|---|---|---|
| **1.** | b | **5.** | a |
| **2.** | b | **6.** | b |
| **3.** | a | **7.** | a |
| **4.** | a | | |

Now that you know a little about the trick solution to the famous puzzle described in number 7, see if you can solve it:

Draw four straight lines (without lifting your pencil from the paper) that cross through all nine dots below.

● ● ●

● ● ●

● ● ●

Answer, page 277

## SIDEWINDERS

## SOMEONE'S KNOCKING

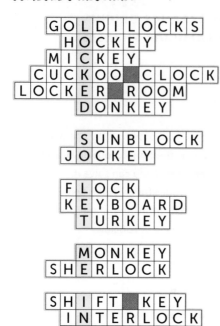

```
G O L D I L O C K S
  H O C K E Y
M I C K E Y
C U C K O O ▮ C L O C K
L O C K E R ▮ R O O M
    D O N K E Y
```

```
S U N B L O C K
J O C K E Y
```

```
F L O C K
K E Y B O A R D
T U R K E Y
```

```
M O N K E Y
S H E R L O C K
```

```
S H I F T ▮ K E Y
  I N T E R L O C K
```

**A:** The knock-knock joke ends: Doris (Door is) LOCKED SO LET ME IN.

## SPEED LIMIT

manatee plugging holes

magician photographing hat

monster parting hair

mummy patching hammock

moose pulling harp

matador paying horse

musicians painting house

motel predicting hurricane

monkey pitching hamburger

mime protecting heart

machine plucking hens

mailman pinching himself

mannequin pouring honey

maid polishing hourglass

mothers playing hopscotch

## SPIN CYCLE

1. PLANET
2. CAROUSEL
3. TORNADO
4. PINWHEEL
5. WHIRLPOOL
6. BALLERINA
7. PROPELLER

## SPLIT DECISION

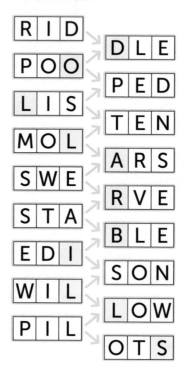

| | |
|---|---|
| R I D | D L E |
| P O O | P E D |
| L I S | T E N |
| M O L | A R S |
| S W E | R V E |
| S T A | B L E |
| E D I | S O N |
| W I L | L O W |
| P I L | O T S |

**A:** DOLLAR BILLS (which become coins when you "break" them)

## SPOONERISMS:
### ROARING PAIN AND POURING RAIN

1. weeping lizards / leaping wizards
2. duck store / stuck door
3. bunny phone / funny bone

## SWEET TALK

GUMDROPS
JAWBREAKER
CANDY CORN
LOLLIPOP
CHOCOLATE
JELLY BEANS

### T: THE PUZZLE

1. TEMPER TANTRUM
2. TREASURE TROVE
3. TEETER-TOTTER
4. TICKET TAKER
5. TONGUE TWISTER
6. TOURIST TRAP
7. TALL TALE
8. TIME TRAVEL
9. TOP TEN
10. TEST TUBE
11. TOW TRUCK
12. TREE TRUNKS

**THE TERMITE'S RESPONSE IS:**

"Yes, but . . . THIS TABLE TASTES TERRIFIC!"

### TASTE-MAKERS

A: FOURTEEN CARROTS (carats)

# TOM FOOLERY:
## TOM SWIFTIES

"The exit is right there," Tom POINTED OUT.

## TRACKING DOWN

(HIDE)
SIDE
SIRE
SORE
SOLE
POLE
PILE
PINE
PINK
PICK
PECK
PEEK
(SEEK)

## TYPE CASTING

| | | | |
|---|---|---|---|
| 1. | e | 6. | b |
| 2. | d | 7. | c |
| 3. | j | 8. | g |
| 4. | i | 9. | a |
| 5. | f | 10. | h |

## U: THE PUZZLE

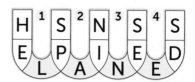

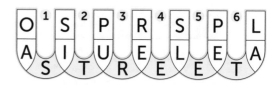

## UDDER CONFUSION

1. HOT THINGS: fire, sun, iron; hot coffee or tea from bottom
2. RED THINGS: heart, fire engine, barn; apple from bottom
3. THINGS THAT GO UP AND DOWN: zipper, window, yo-yo; seesaw from bottom
4. THINGS THAT START WITH V: vulture, volcano, violin; vase from bottom
5. THINGS THAT RHYME WITH "AIR": square, chair, bear; pear from bottom

## UNDERCOVER ASSIGNMENT

**BONUS MESSAGE:** Spies helped George Washington defeat the British.

## UNITED NATIONS

1. Spain (it's **pain**ful)
2. Brazil (ze**bra zil**lions)
3. Germany (ea**ger many**)
4. Japan (nin**ja pan**ted)
5. Egypt (strat**egy Pt**olemy)
6. Canada (**can a da**y)
7. India (**in dia**ries)
8. Portugal (tri**p or tug a l**ot)
9. Norway (take**n or way**)
10. Denmark (hid**den mark**etplace)
11. Panama (**u**p an **ama**zing)
12. China (lun**ch in a**ny)

## UPS AND DOWNS: LET'S LOOK AT AMBIGRAMS ANOTHER WAY

NOON

## V: THE PUZZLE

1. ice, alley
   (vice, valley)
2. culture, local, ease (vulture, vocal, vase)
3. five (in Roman numerals, V=5)
4. seen (seven)
5. valve (value)
6. of
7. revival, divisive, survive (real, die, sure)
8. revolver

A: FLYING GEESE (which often fly in the shape of a V)

## VAMPIRE BATCH

**DIFFERENCES:**

1. Cape comes down farther.
2. Tooth is forward.
3. Mirror is shorter.
4. Comb is longer.
5. Cape is missing points around shoulders.
6. (Match)
7. Index finger is extended instead of pinkie.
8. Forward leg is moved.

## VARIETY SHOW

### THE ORDER OF THE ACTS IS:

1. Magic
2. Dog act
3. Juggling
4. Acrobatics
5. Singing

## VEG OUT

1. PERHAPS (peas)
2. POLICE STATION (potato)
3. ACCORDION (corn)
4. CELEBRITY (celery)
5. BLUE JEANS (beans)
6. OPINION (onion)
7. AUTOMATON (tomato)
8. SQUEAMISH (squash)
9. PICKER-UPPER (pepper)

## VROOM SERVICE

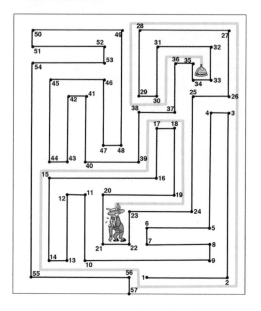

# VISUAL TRICKERY:
## AND OPTICAL ILLUSIONS

B, which is a *Möbius strip*. A Möbius strip has one continuous side—if you put your finger in one spot on the strip and then move around the strip without lifting your finger, you'll end up in the same spot after touching both sides of the strip. You can make a Möbius strip by taking a strip of paper, giving it a half-twist, and taping or gluing the ends together.

## W: THE PUZZLE

*WINDY*  *WARFARE*

*writer*  *wizard*

*Weddings*  *WEALTH*

**WRECK**  WILD WEST

WINTER

## WEAVING A SPELL

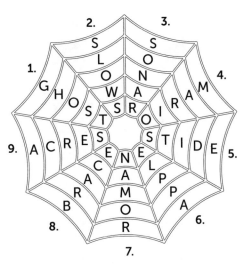

## WHAT'S THE BUZZ?

| D | R | A | W |
|---|---|---|---|
| R | I | C | H |
| A | C | H | E |
| W | H | E | Y |

| S | O | F | T |
|---|---|---|---|
| O | B | O | E |
| F | O | U | R |
| T | E | R | M |

A: YOU MUST START FROM SCRATCH.

## WAY TO GO!

269

## WHICH IS WHICH?

**MONKEY**

**APE**

**PORTRAIT**

**LANDSCAPE**

**STALACTITE**

**STALAGMITE**

**TORNADO**

**HURRICANE**

**PUPIL**

**IRIS**

**LONGITUDE**

**LATITUDE**

**TRICERATOPS**

**STEGOSAURUS**

**REPUBLICAN**

**DEMOCRAT**

**HOUR HAND**

**MINUTE HAND**

**NUT**

**BOLT**

## WHITE HOUSE TOUR

1. Richard Nixon
2. Ronald Reagan
3. Abraham Lincoln
4. Theodore Roosevelt
5. Bill Clinton
6. Barack Obama

## WILD WEST

```
Y O B W O C C P H I T T O N S
N L Y H K A A L C R E I N S E
I L A D C L W N N X S S E T L
A T U T O A M R A I L R O A D
R S U M R E O S R M P D U M D
T S I B R O N C O X W E J P A
N N E R A T T L E S N A K E S
O S S A L I A Y G G I H L D T
G E R T A H N O L L A G N E T
A E O N M O A C O Y O T E O N
W T H A P P Y T R A I L S H S
```

**FASCINATIN' FACT:**
It only lasted eighteen months.

## WINDOW DRESSING

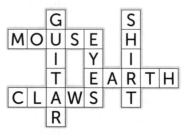

**A:** The costumer is always right.

## WORD ORIGINS: STRANGE ETYMOLOGIES

"God be with you" eventually turned into "good-bye."

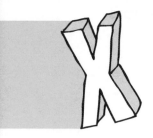

## X: THE PUZZLE

1. tax, tacks
2. rex, wrecks
3. tux, tucks
4. flex, flecks
5. sax, sacks
6. lynx, links
7. wax, whacks
8. Knox, knocks

## X GAMERS

**RABIA:** bicycle
**STEPHEN:** motocross bike
**TERRENCE:** snowmobile
**UMA:** car
**VERNON:** striped snowboard
**WEN:** plain snowboard

## XI FACTS ABOUT XWORD PUZZLES

Scrabble

## X MARKS THE SPOT

1.

2.

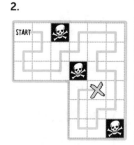

3.

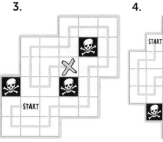

4.

## X-RAY VISIONS

### DIFFERENCES:

1. Hip X-ray shows extra vertebrae.
2. Jar on counter isn't shown as X-ray.
3. Dog has extra ear.
4. (Match)
5. Bottom of doctor's coat has narrower opening.
6. Dog's tail doesn't wag as far.

## Y: THE PUZZLE

1. SAND + CRAB + Y = CANDY BARS
2. TOP + NAIL + Y = PONYTAIL
3. DIME + ANT + Y = DYNAMITE
4. TAPE + FINS + Y = SAFETY PIN
5. SCALE + RAKE + Y = LAYER CAKES
6. PAINTING + ARMS + Y = PRAYING MANTIS
7. DIRT + SACK + Y = YARDSTICK

## YAKKITY YAK

### PREHISTORIC ANIMALS

saber-toothed tiger
triceratops
Tyrannosaurus rex
woolly mammoth
velociraptor
stegosaurus
pterodactyl

### SCIENTISTS AND INVENTORS

Thomas Edison
Albert Einstein
Jane Goodall
Benjamin Franklin
Isaac Newton
Marie Curie
George Washington Carver

### MYSTERY LIST: DOG BREEDS

Labrador Retriever
German Shepherd
Basset Hound
Border Collie
Cocker Spaniel
Siberian Husky
French Poodle

## YARD WORK

(YARD)
CARD
CORD
CORE
CONE (traffic cone)
CANE
CASE (guitar case)
BASE
BALE (bale of hay)
(SALE)

## YEAR IN, YEAR OUT

JANITOR

LIFEBOAT

YELLOW SUBMARINE

APRON

MAYOR

JUNGLE GYM

ROMEO AND JULIET

DAUGHTER

SURPRISE PARTY

NOCTURNAL

MAN OVERBOARD

TOOTH DECAY

## YO HO HO

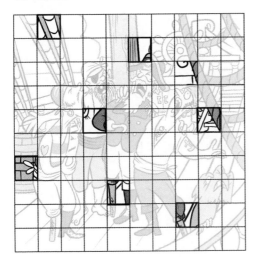

**A:** They get STUCK ON THE HIGH C'S (seas).

## YOU MUST REMEMBER THIS:
### MNEMONIC DEVICES

The correct spelling is PRIVILEGE. The mnemonic is a reminder that the first two vowels are both "I" and the last part contains the letters L–E–G.

## YUCK!

| H | O | S | T |
|---|---|---|---|
| E | R | I | E |
| L | E | G | S |
| D | O | N | T |

**A:** GETTING HIT IN THE NOSE.

# Z: THE PUZZLE

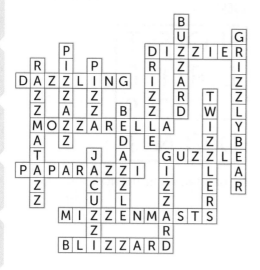

## ZANY BRAINIES

1. CHEAP SHEEP
2. HIKING VIKING
3. FLIPPER ZIPPER
4. SATURN PATTERN
5. CANDLE HANDLE
6. PEPPERED LEOPARD
7. SOLAR STROLLER
8. BALLOON SALOON

# ZEUS RETURNS TO SUEZ:
## A LOOK BACK AT REVERSALS

DESSERTS ("stressed" backward)

## ZIGS AND ZAGS

1.

2.

3.

4.

5.

6.

## ZOM-BEES

1. dandelion, lilac, pansy
2. violet, lily, buttercup
3. orchid, poppy, daffodil
4. snapdragon, daisy, rose
5. crocus, tulip, marigold
6. carnation, azalea, iris

## ZIP LINE

A: He heard they were giving out tickets.

## ZOODOKU

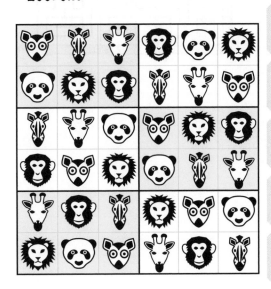

## Z YOU LATER

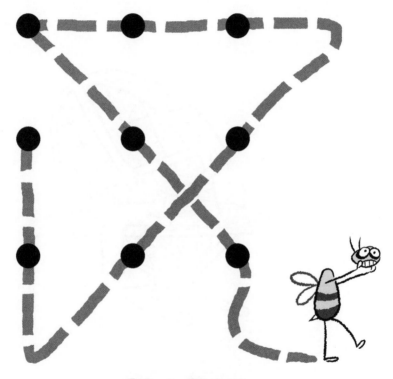

**SO LONG!**